Sharpening Made Easy

A Primer on Sharpening Knives and Other Edged Tools

by Steve Bottorff

Sharpening Made Easy:
A Primer on Sharpening Knives and Other Edged Tools
by Steve Bottorff

second printing, 2005

ISBN 0-940362-19-8

Published in the United States of America by
Knife World Publications
P.O. Box 3395, Knoxville, TN 37927
Phone: 1-800-828-7751
www.knifeworld.com

Dedication and Acknowledgements

I dedicate this book to the memory of my grandfather Dr. Charles M. Bottorff, who got me started; and my wife Patricia, who saw it through to the finish.

Special thanks to Cliff Stamp, Joe Talmadge, Alvin in Arizona, Ching Lee, and Webb Collings for reviewing sections of the manuscript. My biggest thanks go to Kim Knott for the drawings, and to Mark Zalesky for being both editor and friend, and for taking most of the photographs in the book.

Thanks also to the EdgeCraft, EdgePro, GATCO, Klawhorn, Lansky, McGowan, Meyerco, Razor Edge Systems, Razor Sharp Edgemaking, Skarb, Spyderco and Tormek companies for their assistance with this project.

Photographic credits: Boker (p. 57), DMT (p. 32, top), EdgeCraft (p. 76), EdgePro (p. 38, bottom), KnifeArt.com (p. 31), Lansky (p. 38, top; p. 45, top; pages 65, 70, 71), Spyderco (p. 32, bottom), Tormek (p. 77).

Table of Contents

Foreword

Sharpening is an apparently simple task, but it eludes many of us, even with practice. Our sharpening efforts don't produce the results we hope for, and sometimes even make the blade duller. We try different sharpeners with mixed results, and usually settle for just using dull knives.

This book will teach you the skills and equipment needed to establish and maintain a sharp edge on pocket, kitchen and sporting knives.

It also contains information on how to sharpen some other household tools. Even basic, inexpensive tools can benefit from sharpening. You may ask why you would want to sharpen something that you can replace for a few dollars. First, knives and kitchen gadgets straight from the manufacturer are rarely as sharp as they could be. Second, you will have the satisfaction of doing it yourself. A $3.00 knife or vegetable peeler can be the raw material you use to make something better.

A sharp knife is a pleasure to use. It is also safer to use than a dull knife. I hope this book brings that pleasure and safety to you.

–S.B., August 2005

NOTE: Some drawings in this book are not to scale, as certain features have been exaggerated for emphasis.

Introduction

What Is Sharpness?

When we pick up an edged tool, we want it to cut. To the cook that means going through a tomato's tough skin without so much pressure that we damage the ripe fruit. To the woodworker it means planing off a thin shaving without damaging the wood. In the field we may want to chop wood or cut a rope, and in front of the mirror every morning we expect a clean shave. Each of these tasks uses a different edged tool, but what they have in common is a sharp edge. Let's look at what makes an edge sharp.

The gold standard for sharpness is the razor blade, so let's take a look at one. If you take a magnifying glass and look at the edge of a single-edged razor blade (the kind used in paint scrapers), the first thing you will notice is the primary bevel. This was ground with a medium stone, about 300 grit, and therefore it is not polished. You will be able to see scratches in it. Looking closer to the edge, you will see a secondary bevel that is polished. Shift the blade

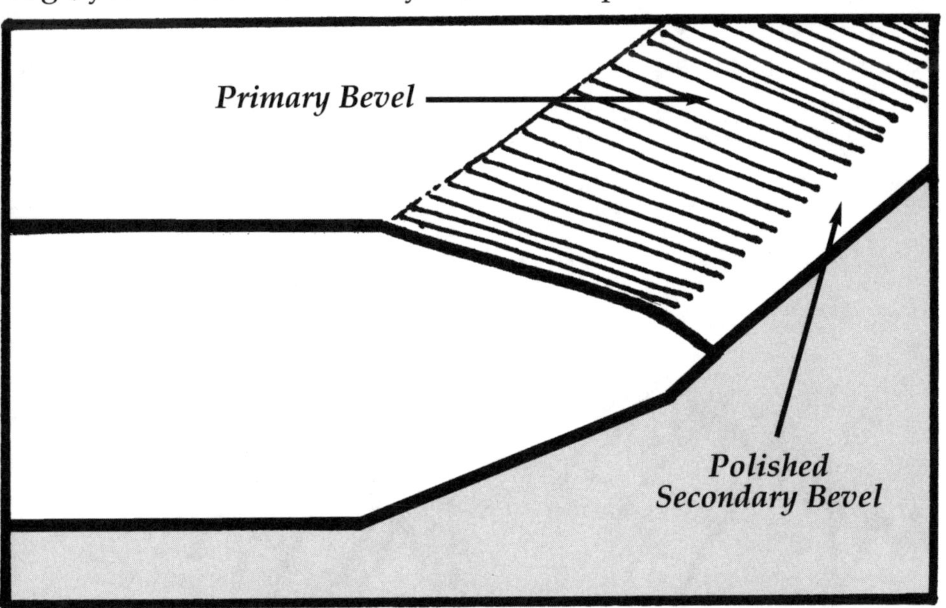

On a razor blade you can see two bevels – a primary bevel and a polished secondary bevel.

and you will see light reflecting off this bevel. It has a mirror finish and was polished by stropping with an extremely fine abrasive. These are the basic conditions we are going to reproduce on a knife blade. We will modify this slightly on other edge tools, depending on the use.

A sharp edge is simply two surfaces or bevels that come together to form an edge. Any edge thickness under a few thousandths of an inch could be considered sharp. Writing paper is about three-thousandths of an inch thick and will cut you if the conditions are right. Ideally the surfaces would come together to make an edge with zero thickness. However, this is limited by several factors. The most fundamental factor is the smoothness of the bevel surfaces.

Surface Finish vs. Sharpness

Except for gross imperfections like burrs, which we will discuss later, the most important issue in sharpness is smoothness of the bevel that forms the edge. You simply cannot have a perfect edge when two rough surfaces come together, and under the high magnification of an electron microscope the resulting edge looks like a mountain range. There is a fundamental relationship between surface finish and sharpness. The following drawings show the differences between the edges that will be produced from medium, fine and extra-fine stones, and after stropping. For actual microscopic photos, see Leonard Lee's book[1].

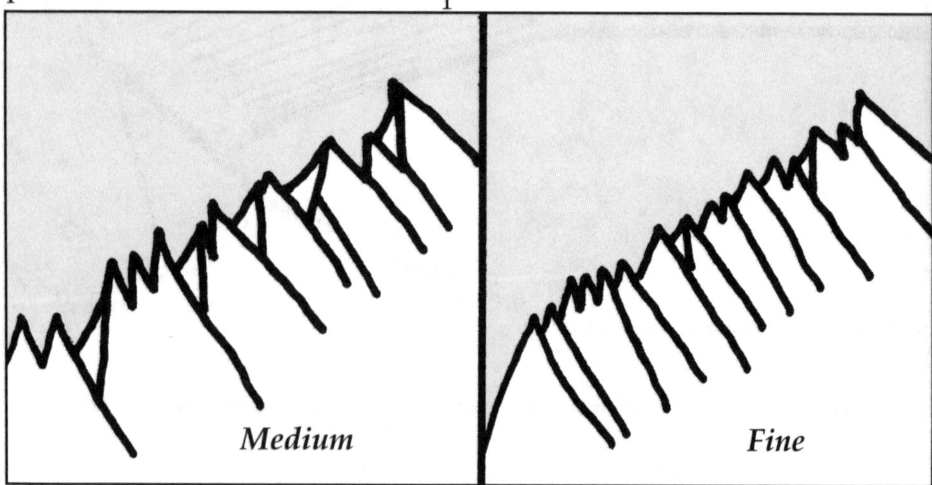

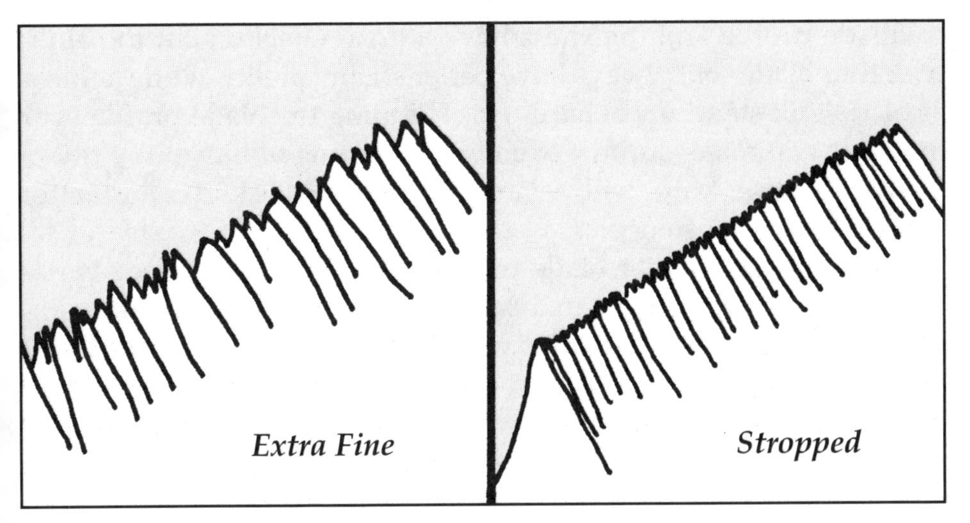

Each finer abrasive used gets closer to the theoretical perfect edge.

Smooth edges are best for cutting most materials and are preferred by barbers, surgeons and woodworkers. Studies by John Juranitch[2] show that butchers can cut more meat and tire less quickly when using a smooth edge. Electron microscope analysis has confirmed that wood cutting ability is correlated to edge smoothness. Sharpening a smooth edge requires more work, but the results are worth it.

That said, there are times when a less than perfect edge is desirable. Blades with a rougher edge can be aggressive cutters because the rough edge acts like a microscopic saw. A rough edge is well suited for slicing fibrous material, such as rope. This edge is easy to produce because you just leave out the final polishing steps. The resulting edge consists of thousands of microscopic sharp peaks that act like microscopic serrations. Blades sharpened this way dull faster as the points wear or bend, so more frequent touch-ups are needed.

Blade Styles

Several other things — blade profile and shape, serrations, etc. — also affect cutting ability. These properties are all determined by the manufacturer, so you want to select each knife with its intended use in mind.

Blade profile and thickness have a great effect on cutting ability. A thin blade will always have better slicing ability, while a thicker blade will stand up to hard use. Thinning the blade profile near the edge can make an improvement in cutting ability, but a thick-bladed hunting knife will never slice like a fillet knife, no matter what you do to the edge.

There are five major blade profiles and dozens of minor variations. Most knives have equal bevels on each side. Some have single bevels. A parallel, flat-sided profile is typical of stamped blades, and is seen on low-cost, high-volume production knives. More expensive forged blades will have a wedge profile. This wedge will typically have slightly convex sides. A truly flat-sided wedge is rare, but is becoming popular in high-end custom knives. A concave or hollow-ground profile is typical of hand-made and custom knives. A flat bevel is a feature of a chisel profile, which has only a single bevel.

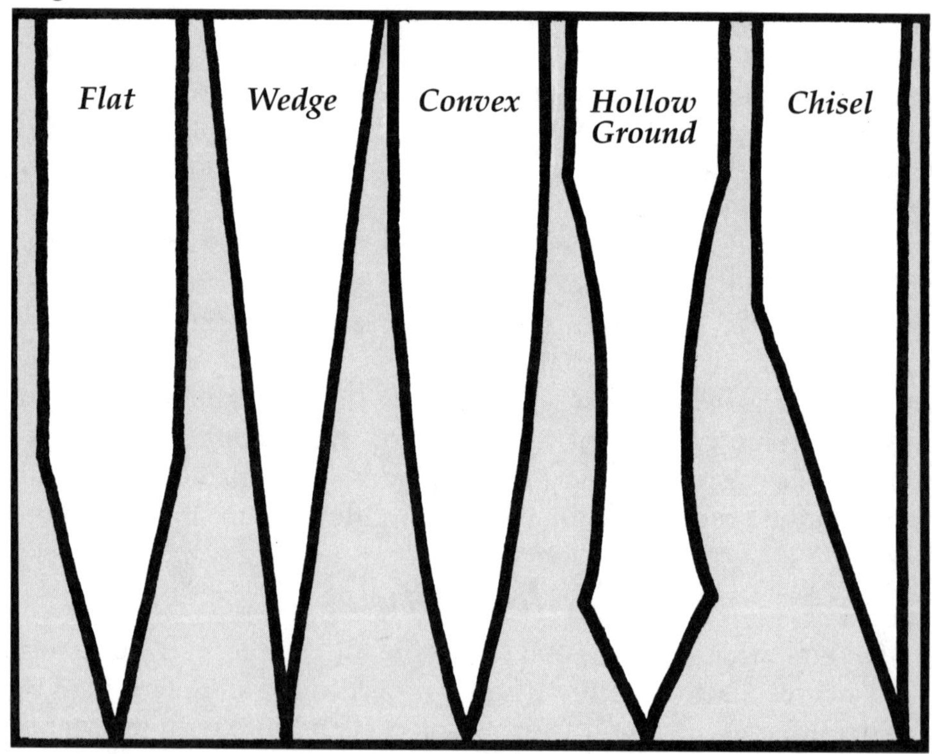

Here are some of the blade profiles you may encounter. Views are cross-sectional.

Blade shape likewise is set when the blade is made and is determined by the usage. For instance, more curve or belly helps skinning and fillet knives slice, while a reverse curve on a linoleum knife allows the tip to be used more effectively.

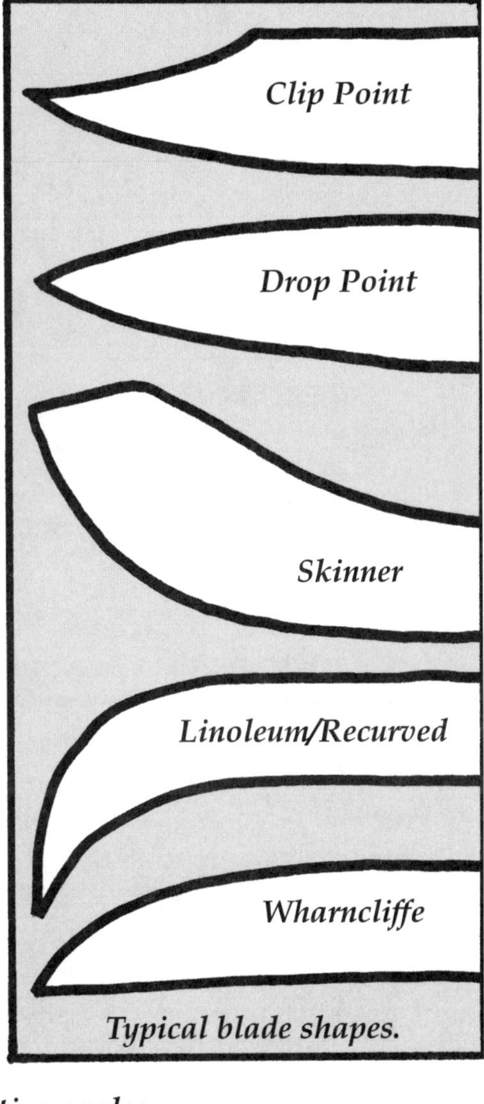

Typical blade shapes.

Serrations help with some cutting chores by letting the edge attack repeatedly from different angles, always slicing the material at a different point. This lets you cut with less pressure. Reverse curves and serrations also give an aggressive look to fantasy knives.

In my opinion serrated edges are best suited for two types of cutting tasks — slicing tender material like tomatoes and bread, and cutting fibrous material like rope. All other tasks are done as well or better with a plain edge. A plain edge is also easier to maintain.

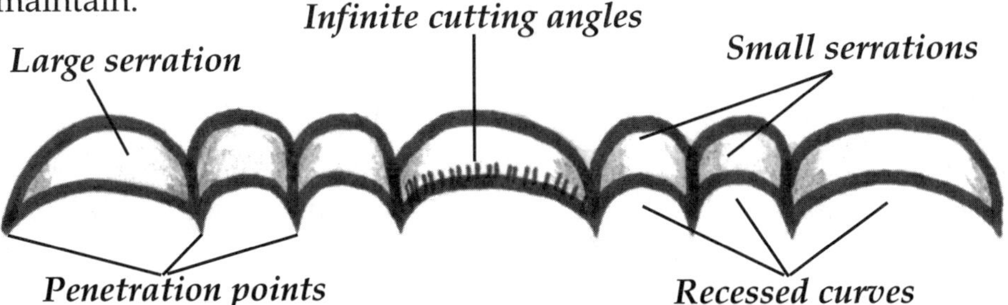

Closeup view of a serrated edge.

Plain edge or serrated? Both have their place.

Edge Profile

The edge profile (the first 1/16 to 1/8 inch from the edge) is independent of the blade style. The edge profile can be convex, flat or concave just like the blade profile. A concave edge is characteristic of certain types of sharpening machines so we need not consider it now. A convex edge is a special case we will discuss later. For now, let's concentrate on the flat bevel edge profile.

Practical edge angles can vary from 10 degrees to 40 degrees. Different angles are suited for different tasks: a small angle as found on our razor blade will slice well, but a thicker angle will hold up longer. Most edge angles are between 18 degrees (fillet knives) and 30 degrees (survival knives). Twenty degrees is about right for kitchen knives, twenty-two degrees is good for pocket knives, and twenty-five degrees gives a long lasting edge to a camp knife. Edge angle is difficult to measure after the fact, but is fairly easy to control when sharpening by controlling the angle between the stone and the blade.

Most western knives are double bevel, so the total angle at the edge is twice the bevel angle. Many woodworking tools and some Asian knives are single bevel. Their total angle is equal to the bevel angle, so it is generally less than that of a double bevel edge. The resulting small angle can make them aggressive but fragile cutters. That is why sashimi knives are so sharp.

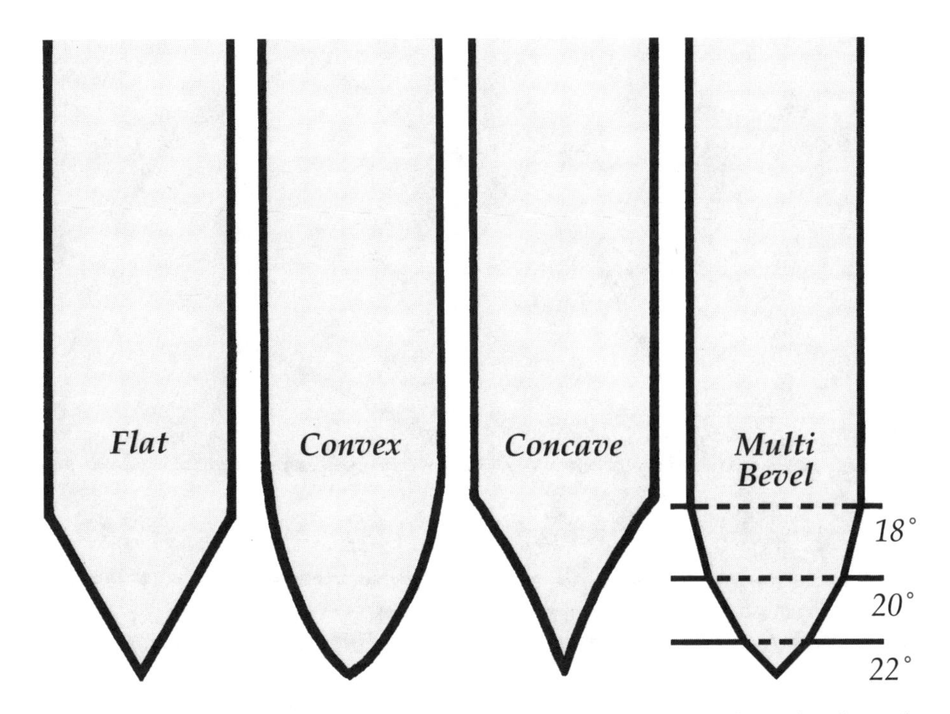

The main edge profiles are flat, convex, concave and multi-bevel. View is cross-sectional.

It is easy to get confused about edge angles. Some makers quote the total angle rather than the bevel angle. If a quoted angle seems high, it may be because of this difference. Edge angle is usually measured from the centerline of the blade, but some systems measure edge angle from one blade side or the other rather than the centerline. This may differ by up to 5 degrees from the angle measured from the centerline. You may read about angles for knives that do not match the angles I cite. This is not important, so don't let it concern you.

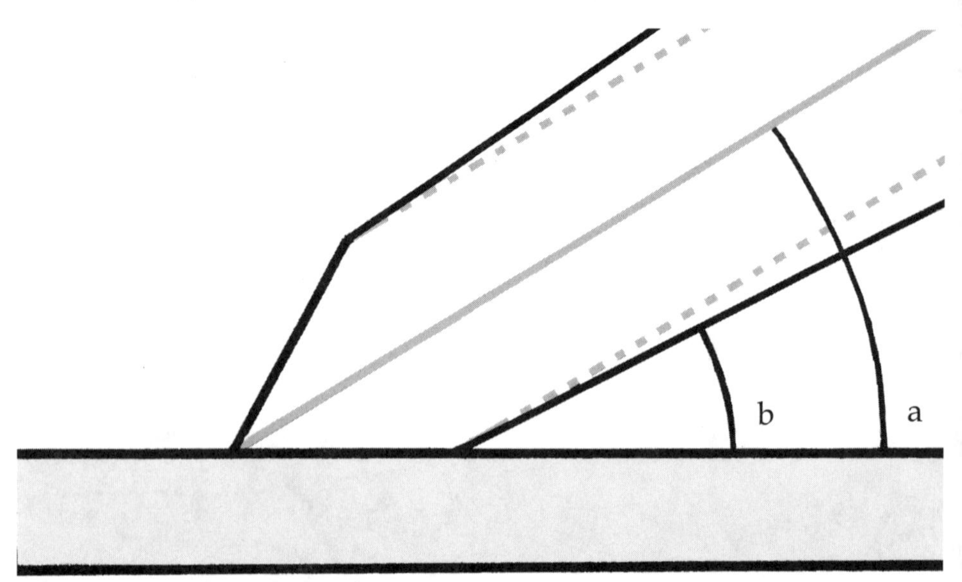

Measuring edge angles from the centerline is most common (a). If measured from the side of a non-parallel sided blade, the angle may differ by up to 5° (b). View is cross-sectional.

The importance of knowing the exact angle has been overemphasized. Knives are functional through a range of angles. **The important thing is to control the angle so you do not end up with a sloppy, rounded over edge.** A good starting point is to duplicate the original angle the maker put on the blade. If the knife does not cut well when sharpened at this angle, consider using a smaller angle when you sharpen it again.

Testing the Edge

To be sure you are improving your sharpening, you need a way to test the results. Test methods can range from cutting silk to chopping trees. Here are several test methods that I think are useful.

Many people test an edge by rubbing their thumb lightly across the edge and feeling how the edge grabs as it tries to cut into the thumb pad. Be very careful, and only test lightly and in a direction perpendicular to the edge. *Never* slide your thumb along the edge. Slicing is a much more effective cutting method than a straight push, and you are more likely to cut yourself.

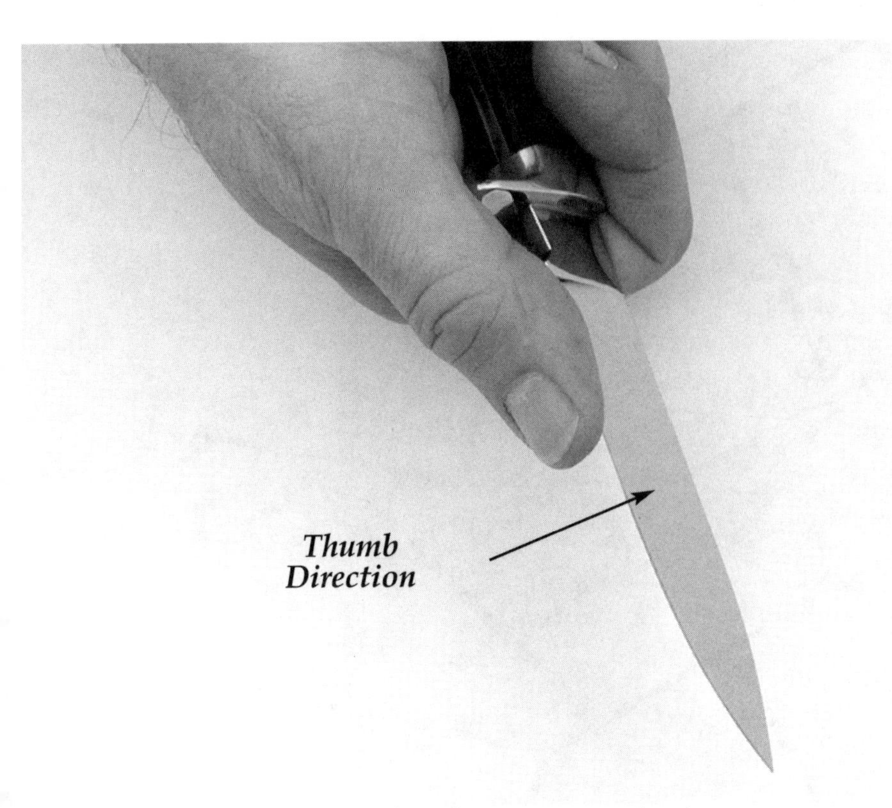

Carefully moving your thumb across an edge is a common test. Never slide your thumb down the edge.

Why, you may ask, is slicing so much more effective? The answer, of course, is that the effective bevel angle is equal to the angle times the cosine of the slicing angle ($x = a \cos b$), but it is easier to explain without the trigonometry. When you come to a steep hill, it is difficult to walk straight up. Instead, you can go up the hill at an angle. The route is longer, but the slope is easier. The same thing happens in slicing. Each fiber being cut must "walk" up the bevel of the edge, and slicing lets them take an easier slope. The longer the slice, the less steep the apparent angle becomes, until it almost disappears. This lets the fairly thick blade in a deli meat slicer cut like a razor. Skew cutting, or cutting at an angle, benefits from the same changes in geometry as slicing, but to a lesser degree.

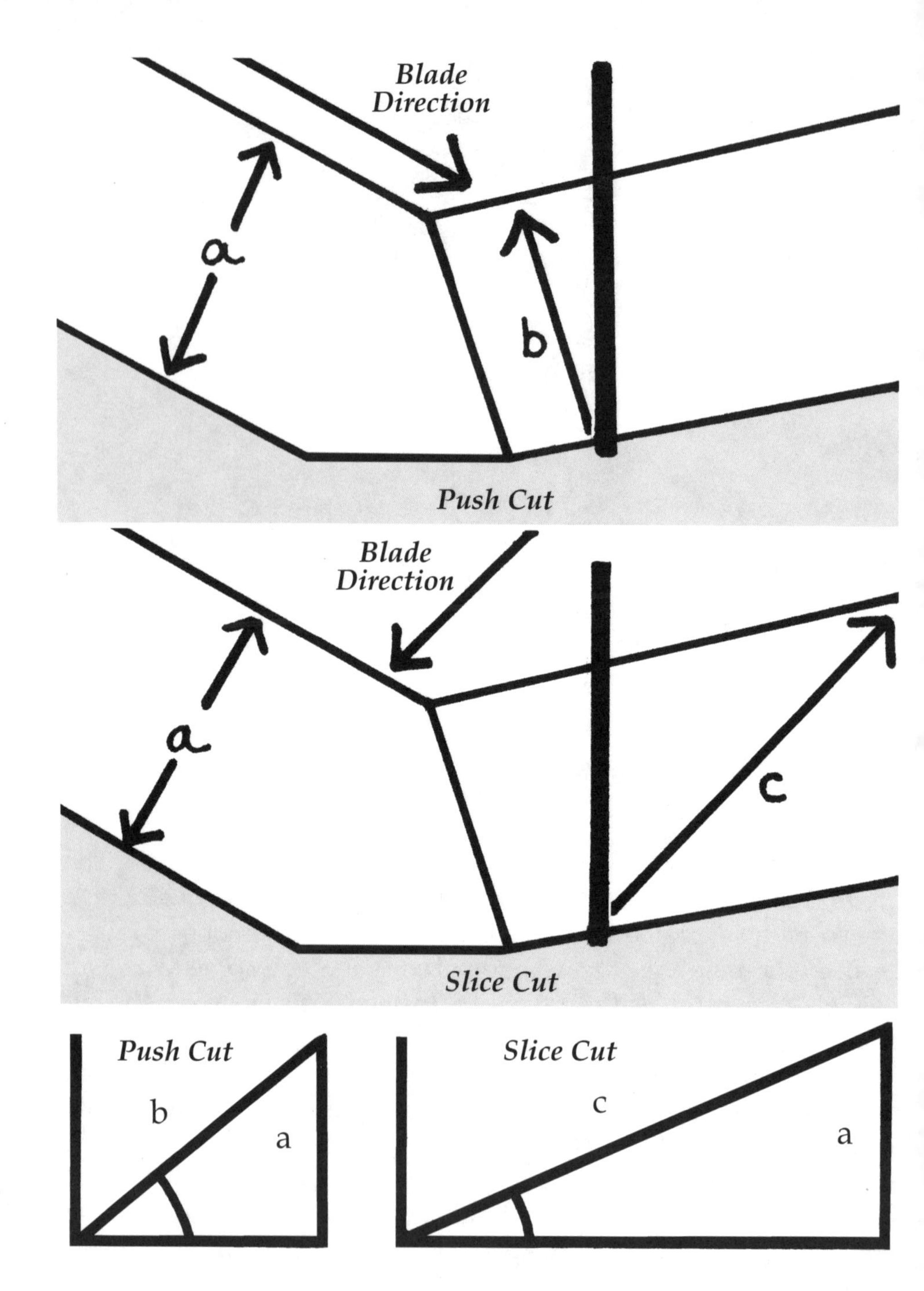

A slicing motion cuts more easily because the apparent bevel angle is reduced.

While with experience you may learn to judge edges by feeling them, it is very subjective. One joke concerns a man who tested sharpness with his tongue. Sharp blades, the story goes, taste like metal, and really sharp blades taste like blood. [Please remember that this is a joke; don't try it.]

We need tests that are more objective.

Slicing a piece of paper is a good test. Use ordinary writing paper; newspaper is a little too soft. Grasp the paper between the thumb and forefinger of your weak hand. Cut downward starting near the heel of the blade and slicing so that you end near the point of the blade. The cut should be at about as long as the blade and use the full length of the blade. As you cut, you can feel any dull spots or nicks as they catch and tear the paper. Paper cutting sharpness is an acceptable sharpness, but it is not as sharp as we can get.

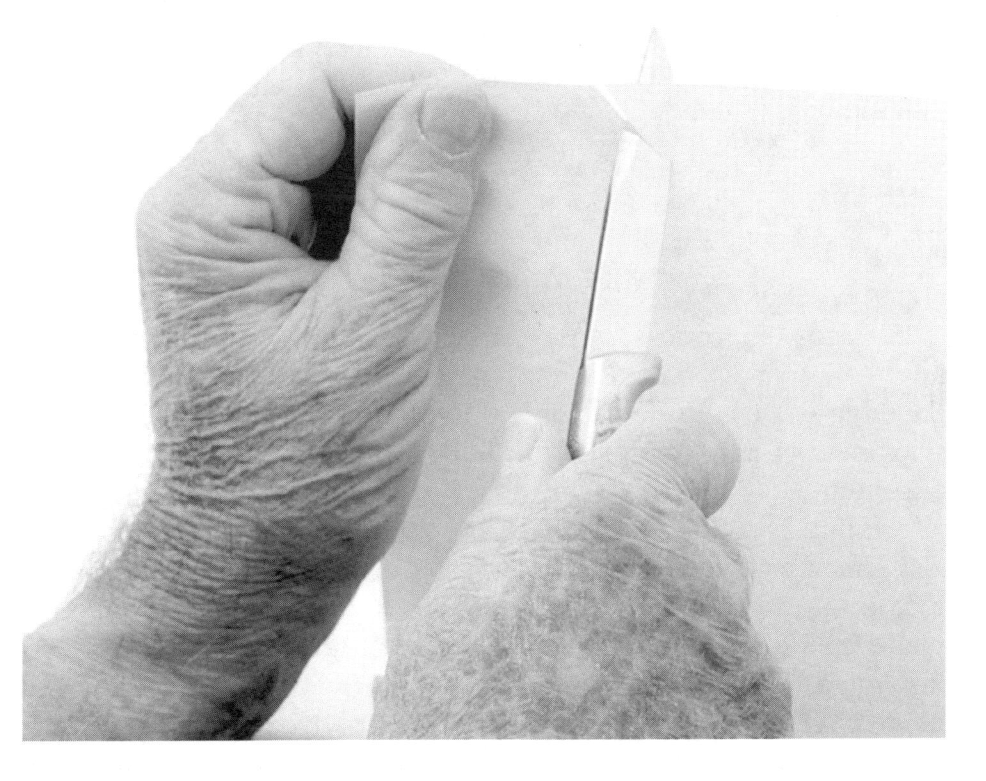

Shaving the hair on your hand or arm is another common sharpness test. It is useful to define two higher levels of sharpness.

If the edge just barely shaves, and perhaps misses some hairs, that is shaving sharpness. Even greater sharpness, comparable to a razor blade or scalpel, will literally pop the hairs off your hand or arm. We will call this razor sharpness.

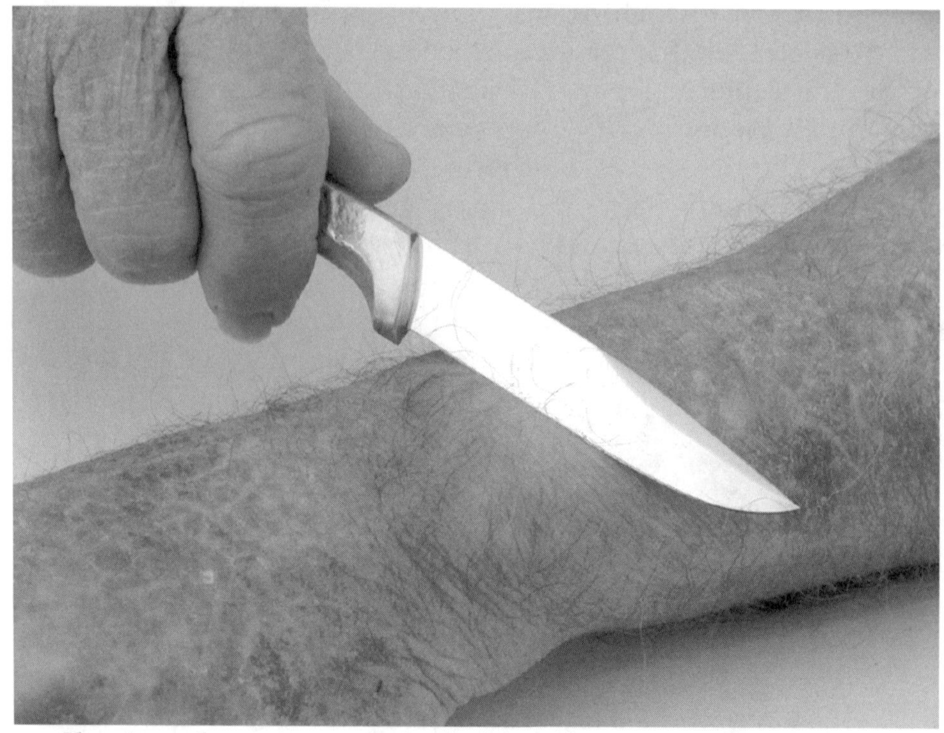

Shaving sharpness can be achieved even on heavy hunting knives or an axe. I have a hunting knife that will shave even though the edge angle is a rather blunt 30-degree bevel on each side. Razor sharpness is only possible with both a polished edge and a small edge angle.

Testing by shaving can be misleading if the blade has a burr, also called a wire edge. Steel naturally forms a burr — a thin bendable projection — on the edge during the sharpening process. A blade with a burr may shave but will not stand up to hard use. To test for a burr, slide your fingertips lightly from the side of the blade over the edge. You will feel the burr drag against your fingers. Test from both sides, because burrs are usually bent over one way or the other. Also, a blade that will shave one way but will not shave going the other way has a burr edge. As your sharpening improves, you will be looking for smaller and smaller burrs.

Many good sharpeners, including my grandfather, have learned

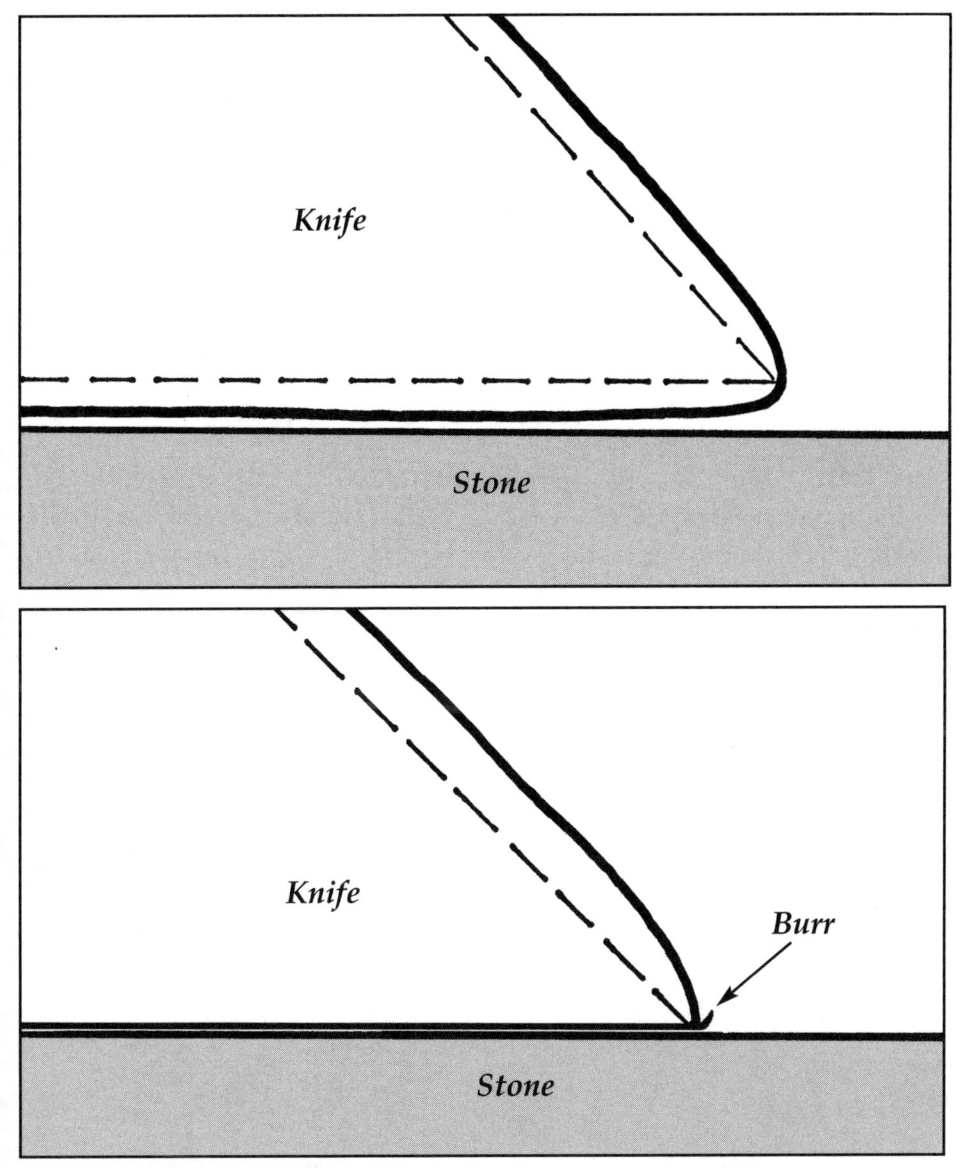

A burr is a natural result of the sharpening process.
View is cross-sectional.

to see a dull edge. Hold the blade in front of you with the edge in line with a bright light. Move the blade around a bit. A dull edge will reflect a glint. Nicks and burrs will also cause glints. When the blade is sharp these glints will be gone.

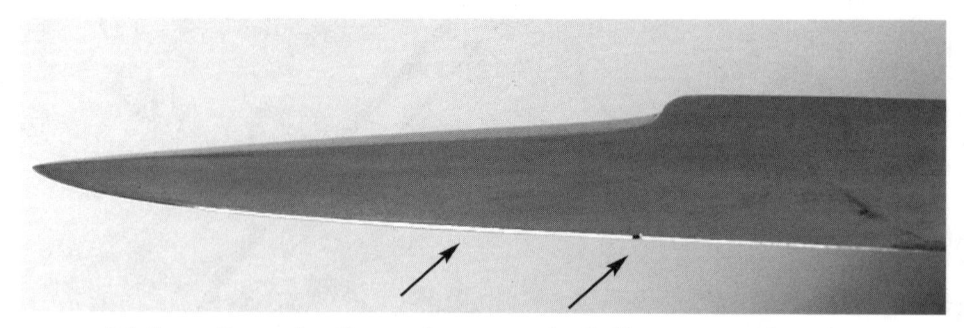

Light reflected off an edge reveals dull areas and nicks.

Another good test for sharpness is to press the edge lightly on your thumbnail at about a 30-degree angle. If it cuts into your nail and stops, it is sharp. If it slips, it is dull. The sharper the blade, the smaller you can make the angle before it slips. Shaving sharp blades start to slip at about 30 degrees; razor sharp blades can go down to 20 degrees or less. Test in several spots along the blade's length. Try this with a new razor blade to see how a really sharp blade acts.

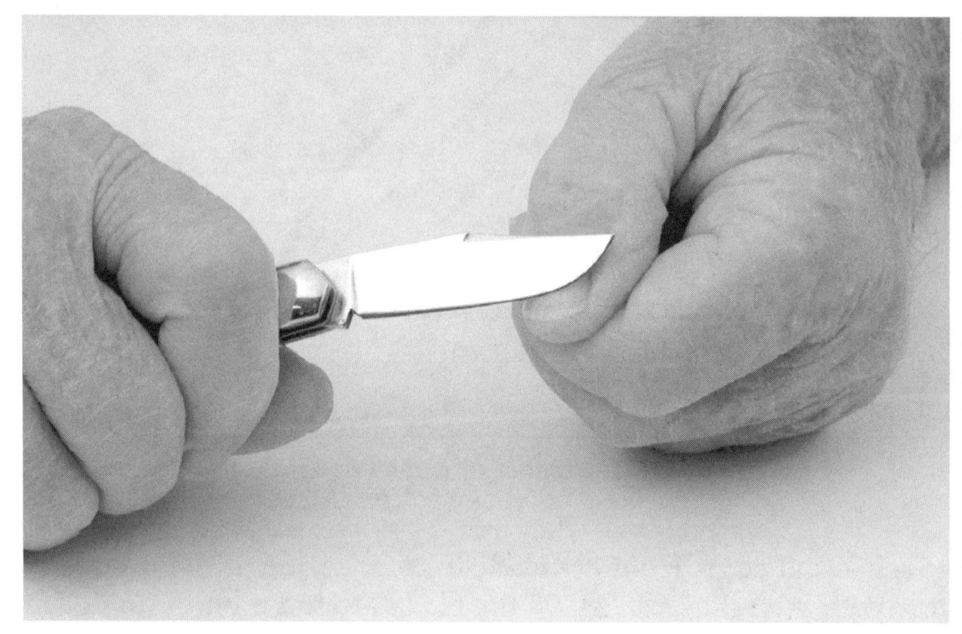

The down side of testing on your thumbnail is that the little cuts in your nail get dirty and look bad until the nail grows out. An alternative is to do this test using a piece of plastic.

Razor Edge Systems sells a plastic rod for testing sharpness with a special shaped tip for testing for roughness. You can do as well by testing sharpness with a plastic pen (same technique as with a fingernail), and testing for roughness by drawing the blade lightly across the edge of an old credit card, feeling for any rough spots.

That was probably too many tests to remember, so just pick the tests you like and stick with them.

Typical Double-bevel Knife Sharpening Angles	
17 - 18 degrees	An extremely sharp, delicate edge for filet knives, razor blades, craft knives, etc.
19 - 20 degrees	A sharp edge for high quality kitchen and pocket knives
21 - 23 degrees	A general purpose edge for most kitchen and pocket knives
24 - 25 degrees	A durable edge for knives that chop – cleavers, hunting and outdoor knives, etc.
30 degrees	A very durable edge for heavy duty. This is also a typical angle for the single bevel of a chisel grind knife.

The Basics

The Keys to Success

The mistakes commonly made in sharpening are *uncontrolled bevel angles, failure to establish a new edge, failure to hone off the burr,* and *leaving the final bevel too rough.*

Some books recommend sharpening as if trying to slice a thin layer or decal off the stone. This is bad advice, and here's why: most people don't hold a constant angle this way. A dull blade requires that you hold the blade at a different angle than a sharp blade when slicing a thin layer. You instinctively raise the blade angle until you feel and see the edge working. The same thing happens when sharpening by hand on a stone. The duller the blade is, the more you have to raise it before you can sense the edge working against the stone. This creates larger edge angles and thicker bevels as time goes on, and the results gradually deteriorate.

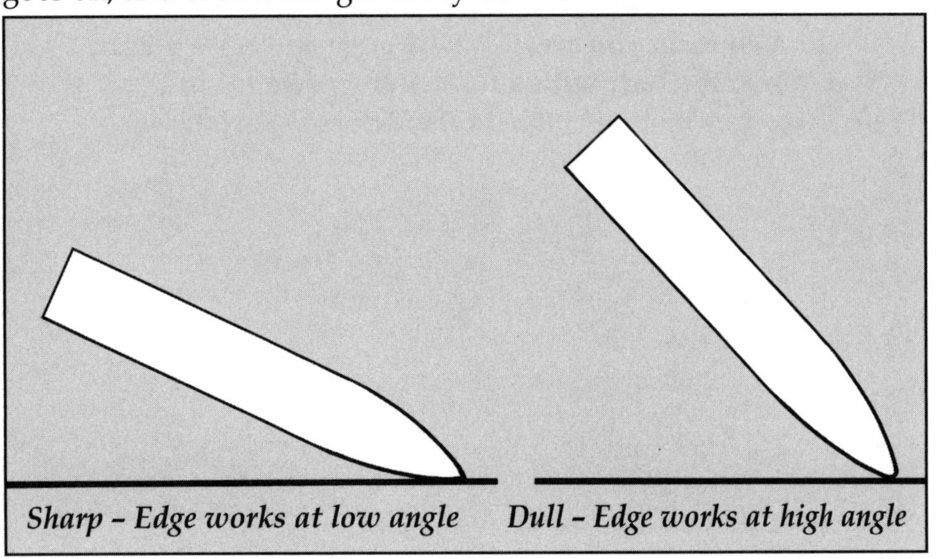

Sharp – Edge works at low angle *Dull – Edge works at high angle*

You have probably heard people complain that the more they sharpen a blade, the duller it becomes. This is not an illusion; it is actually what happens if you follow your instincts and raise the blade angle until the edge meets the stone. Skill and practice can overcome this problem, but the sure-fire way is to use a guide to maintain a consistent edge angle. Guides also produce a better looking result than freehand sharpening.

If you do not remove enough metal to create a new edge, you will leave some of the dull edge in place. The easiest way to determine that you have removed enough metal is to sharpen until you have raised a burr. Steel will naturally form a burr when one bevel is ground until it meets another. It acts as a telltale sign to let us know we have created a new edge. Finer stones produce smaller burrs, but they are still there.

We will develop a technique that produces a small burr so that we do not remove too much metal and shorten the knife's useful life. We will then remove the burr in the honing process and have a sharp edge every time. A final stropping or polishing will bring the edge to perfection.

The keys to success are:
1) Use an angle guide to control the edge angle,
2) Sharpen until you create a new edge and raise a burr,
3) Remove the burr with a finer stone or hone, and
4) Strop or polish the edge to the desired sharpness.

The More I Sharpen, the Duller It Gets!

A sharp blade will pare or whittle at a very low angle, as shown in (A). We have to raise it just enough to create a clearance angle so that the bevel does not ride on the material. As the edge wears, we have to raise the blade to maintain the clearance angle (B). When the blade gets even duller, we raise it still higher in an attempt to bring any remaining edge against the material (C).

When we finally sharpen our blade, the tendency is to sharpen at about the same angle that was last useful (D). In a fairly short time we can sharpen a new edge and everything seems okay. But as this process is repeated, the sharpening angle gets larger and larger, and the width of the cutting edge gets wider ($E_{1,2,3}$). Our edge has become blunt and wide by following the old advice of "trying to scrape a decal off of the stone."

What we must do to restore an effective edge is to sharpen back to the original low angle (F). This removes more metal and takes more time, but there is no alternative. Sharpening properly can be done freehand, but using a guide is our best assurance that we don't unintentionally raise the angle.

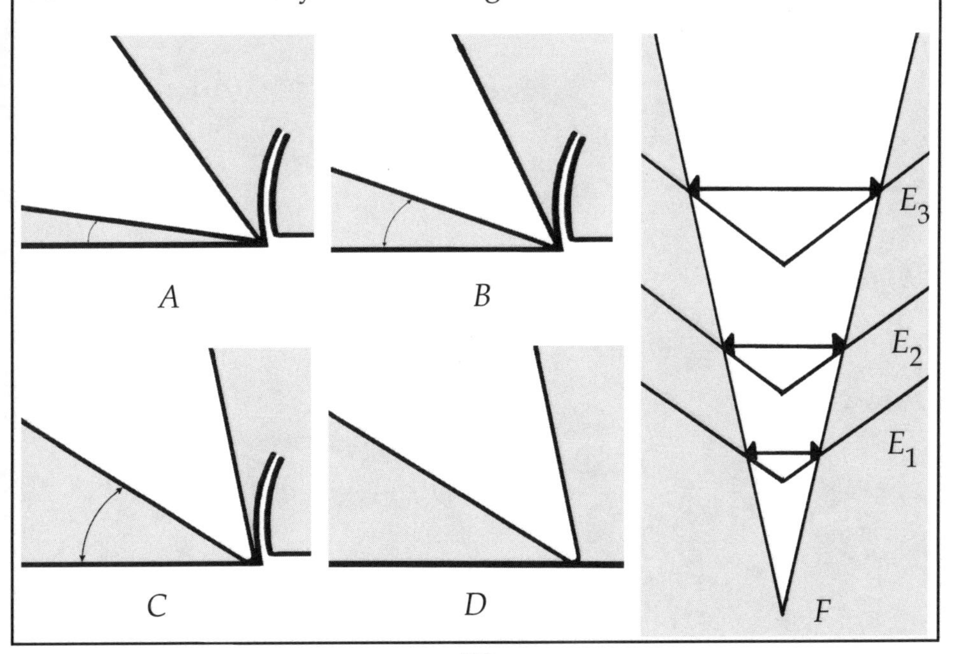

Basic Sharpening Equipment

Selecting a Sharpening System

Every sharpening system or method consists of abrasives, usually stones, but perhaps a wheel or a belt, and a method of guiding and moving the abrasive across the blade, even if it is freehand. You may find that you want to own two or more systems to meet different needs. This book discusses several types of systems, each with their own advantages and drawbacks. Here is a quick summary of their features:

Bench stones: You will never go wrong owning some large rectangular sharpening stones, called bench stones. They traditionally are used freehand, and this method is still preferred by some purists, but they can also be used with an angle guide. Operation is slow, about 5 to 10 minutes per knife. Even if you settle on another system for most of your sharpening, there are several tasks that can only be done with bench stones.

Waterstones: A variation on bench stones is Japanese waterstones. These are much faster cutting than western stones and produce a finer edge. A complete system will include a water bath and a holder for the stones. More technique is required with waterstones – they must be soaked and, because they wear quickly, they must be flattened more often than other stones. This is the system of choice for Japanese knives and tools, and it is gaining popularity among woodworkers.

Basic clamp-on guides: This type of guide is designed for use with bench stones or waterstones. They are relatively inexpensive, especially if you already own some sharpening stones you want to use. They have a limited range of sharpening angles, and you have to reclamp the blade to change the angle.

Rod-guided systems: These are complete systems that use their own small stones. They are very popular because of their ability to put a well-defined bevel on a knife blade. People who value this "like-new" appearance as well as a sharp edge favor them. There is some setup involved, and sharpening takes 5 to 10 minutes per blade. Chose one with a large selection of sharpening angles.

Crock sticks: Vee shaped ceramic rod sharpeners, called crock sticks, are quick to set up and use. Time is 2 to 3 minutes per blade. The better sets have more than one set of rods. Crock sticks are wonderful in the kitchen for quick touch-ups, 1 minute or less.

Slot devices: Various slot devices promise a sharp edge in seconds. There are several cases where they are useful, but none of them is a good general-purpose solution.

Electric Sharpeners: There are several good electric sharpeners on the market. Prices start at under $100 for household units and several semi-professional units are priced under $500. Acceptable electric sharpeners feature several stages, the final stage being a stropping or polishing stage. Avoid single stage units.

I suggest you read this entire chapter on equipment and the chapter titled *Other Sharpening Equipment* before buying. Several different methods are discussed, and each uses a different kind of stone. Reading first may save you from a costly mistake.

Abrasives

Before we discuss equipment further, let's take a look at abrasives.

Natural abrasives are found in both natural and man-made stones. The original "Washita" and "Arkansas" stones were quarried natural stones, but now many stones sold by these names are reconstructed. The abrasive material is novaculite, a mineral related to flint and quartz containing mainly silicon dioxide. The relative hardness of novaculite is only 6.5 on the Mohs scale, the scale developed for minerals and gems. That is just a bit harder than file steel. The original Japanese waterstones were also natural stones.

Natural abrasives work well enough on carbon steel knives, but they struggle with harder tool steels and tougher wear-resistant and stainless steels. For modern steels I recommend stones made with manufactured abrasives or industrial diamonds.

Aluminum oxide, which has a Mohs hardness of 9.2, is also

This set of three man-made stones is a good option for the home sharpener.

bonded to form man-made stones. The bond may either be resin (modern Japanese waterstones), vitrified (India™) or ceramic. Originally this material was also obtained from natural sources (emery and corundum), but artificial aluminum oxide or alumina was developed over a hundred years ago and has all but replaced the natural material.

Japanese waterstones deserve another paragraph because of their special characteristics. Waterstones are second only to diamond hones in cutting speed, and the finest waterstone creates the sharpest edge possible from a stone. These properties come at some sacrifice of other properties. Waterstones wear relatively fast, and need to be flattened every so often.

Silicon carbide is a man-made abrasive material also developed just before 1900. It has a Mohs hardness of 9.4. Stones made from it, such as Norton's Crystolon™, will sharpen almost anything except carbide tools.

Industrial diamonds are made into hones by bonding them to steel, and are therefore sometimes called diamond files. Diamond has a Mohs hardness of 10. Two very different types of diamonds are used in diamond hones. Monocrystalline diamond hones last longer because the diamonds do not fracture readily. Polycrystalline

Diamond hones maintain perfect flatness and will sharpen anything.

diamond hones are less expensive. Diamond hones shoud be used with light pressure to prevent unseating the diamonds.

Ceramic stones are made from aluminum oxide or silicon carbide in a ceramic bond. Ceramic bench stones maintain their flatness very well.

Ceramic benchstones are a great choice for steel knives and tools.

Finer Abrasives

There is a limit to how fine an abrasive can be incorporated into a stone or solid form. That limit is about 1000 grit or 9 microns, and is found in extra-fine diamond hones and the finest hard Arkansas stones. Japanese waterstones have abrasives about this same size, but their shape and the slurry they form makes them cut as if they were smaller – 3 to 5 microns. Automotive finishing sandpapers and micron graded sanding belts are available in this range, too. To go beyond this grit level and get a smoother edge we have to use honing and polishing compounds. These are used on a flexible carrier material such as a leather strop or a buffing wheel. Since these soft carriers can be cut by a sharp edge we *always* strop off (away from) the edge to prevent cutting into the soft carrier material. This is especially important with power stropping and buffing, where the moving wheel or belt can catch and throw the knife, causing injury.

Sharpening Stones

Sharpening stones come in a large variety of sizes and shapes. Many of these are for special uses. You may already own some sharpening stones. For general sharpening the most useful stones are large flat bench stones, at least two of them in different grits. A medium stone and a fine stone are the minimum. An extra fine will produce a sharper edge, and a coarse stone may be needed to sharpen a damaged or neglected blade.

If you do decide on a set of bench stones, I recommend buying the largest ones you can afford. Whether you sharpen with a guide as I suggest below, or sharpen freehand, bigger is better. A 6-inch stone is the smallest you should consider, and an 8-inch is preferable. A 10-inch or larger stone gives you bragging rights as a serious sharpener. Consider one of the sets with three stones mounted in a triangle. They can be rotated on the base to bring each stone into position. Some of these include an oil bath.

For freehand sharpening, the ideal stone would be about as long as the longest knife you plan to sharpen. This will allow the entire edge to be sharpened with a long slicing stroke. Remember that the cook probably owns the really big knives around the house, and you will be expected to sharpen their 8 or 10-inch butcher knives. Smaller stones are handy for field use. There are several suppliers listed in the appendices. Hardware stores and restaurant suppliers are also good sources for sharpening stones.

An inexpensive alternative to stones is silicon carbide sandpaper. A piece of silicon carbide sandpaper (also called "wet-or-dry" sandpaper) glued to a wooden block or piece of plate glass will work as well as a stone. Silicon carbide sandpaper on plate glass is popular with woodworkers for sharpening plane irons and chisels. The finest grades of wet-or-dry sandpaper are used between coats of automobile paints, and can be purchased at auto parts stores.

Cutting Speed vs. Sharpness

Different abrasives sharpen at different rates, and produce different levels of sharpness. The following chart shows this relationship for the most popular sharpening stones.

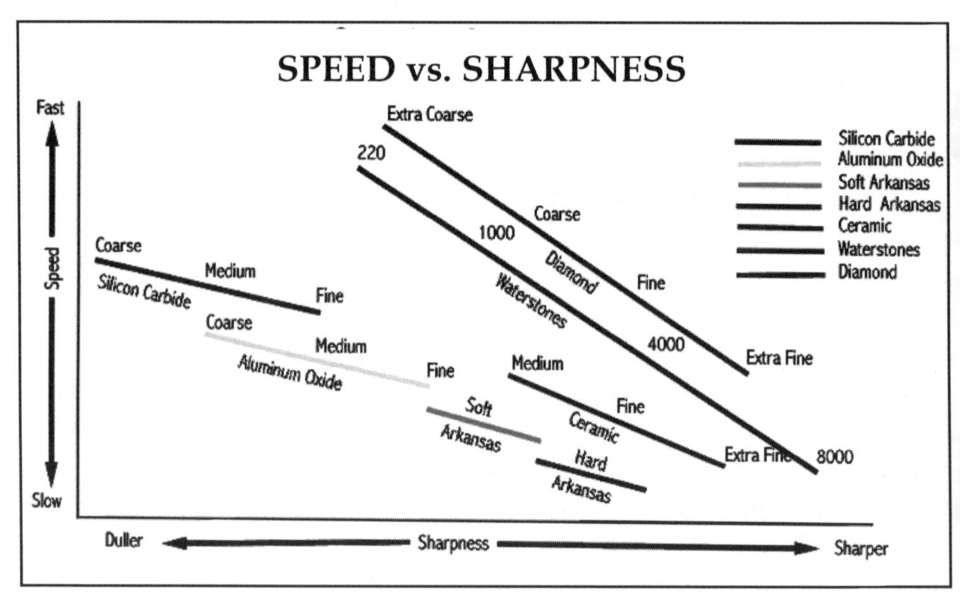

Different abrasives cut at different speeds and produce differing sharpnesses. This chart is available in color at http://users.ameritech.net/knives/speed.htm

Oil vs. Water on Stones

Natural stones tend to clog without oil or water, while most man-made stones can be used dry. In North America we usually use oil on all sharpening stones. Much of the rest of the world uses water. Tests by John Juranitch[2] show that the best results are obtained with a dry stone. Apparently particles carried in the oil dull the edge. I prefer ceramic stones and diamond hones used dry, and my second choice is Japanese waterstones.

I'll leave this up to your personal preference, with the following guidance:

Aluminum oxide and bonded Arkansas stones can be used with oil or dry. Clean them with paint thinner. Ceramic stones and diamond hones can be used with water or dry. Clean them with water and scouring powder when necessary. Washita and natural Arkansas stones can be used with oil or water, and cleaned as described above.

Use and clean Japanese waterstones only with water, but store them dry and soak them before using. (If you prefer to store them wet, protect them from freezing. *Never* add antifreeze to the water, it dissolves the bonding material.)

If you have used water on a stone and want to change to oil, let it dry thoroughly, and then oil it. Once you have used oil on a stone, it is difficult to change back.

Guides

A sharpening guide controls the angle you sharpen at. Guides for use with bench stones clamp on the back of the blade and slide or roll along the stone. The drawback of most of these guides is that they waste up to 3 inches of the stone's length. If you mount your stone flush with your work surface, you can utilize the full stone length. One type of guide moves along the workbench and eliminates this problem. Guides are available not only for knives, but also for chisels and plane irons.

The Skarb guide is unique in that it holds the blade in a clamp that swivels over a standard bench stone. Blades more than twice the length of the stone can be sharpened without moving the clamp.

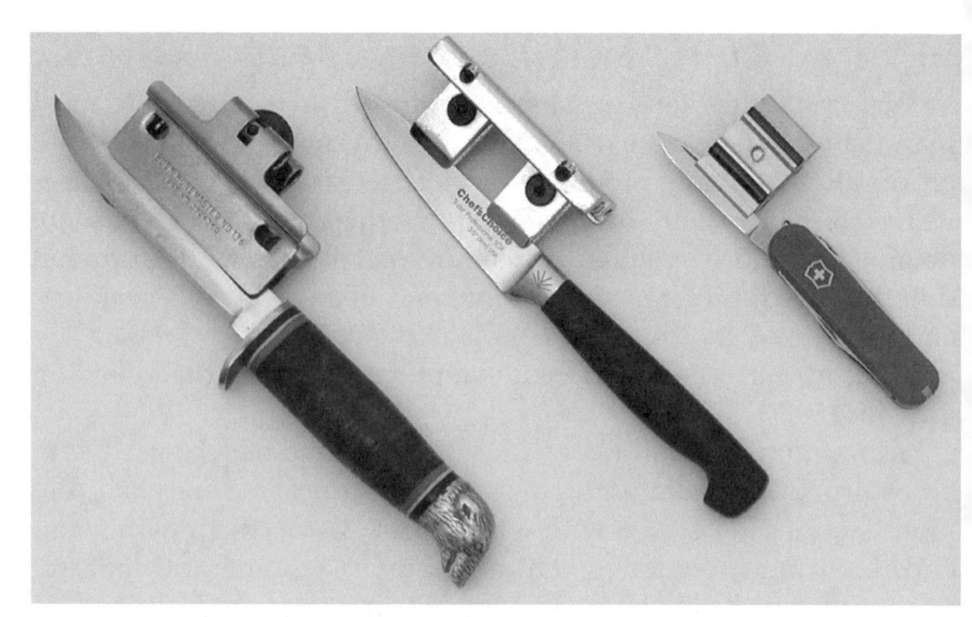

These sharpening guides provide angle control when used with bench stones.

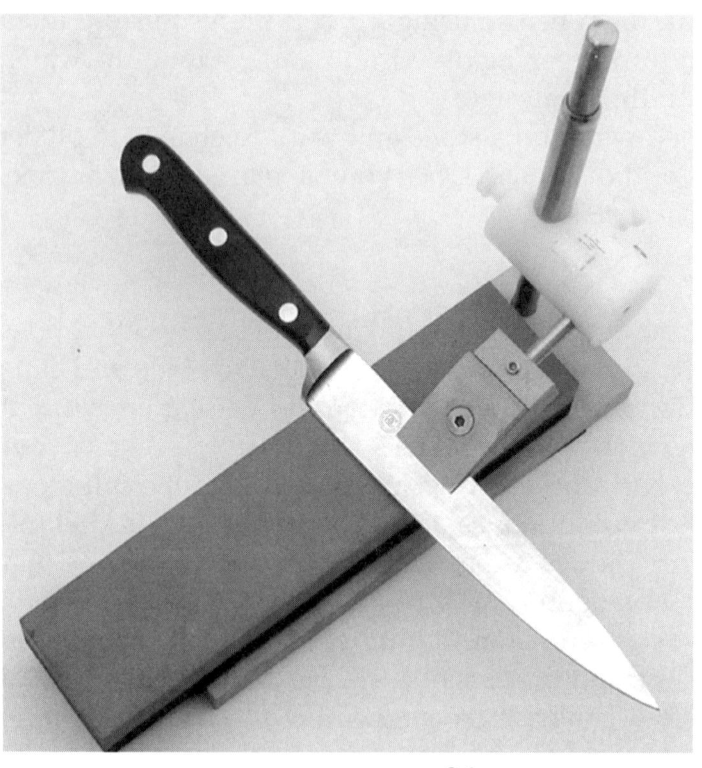

The Skarb is an interesting sharpening guide that uses bench stones.

Rod-Guided Systems

Rod-guided systems come with their own stones, which have a rod attached that slides through a hole or slot in the guide. This controls the angle and also prevents scratching the blade with the stone. Since the guide slides on the rod and not on the stone, a smaller stone is needed. Rod-guided systems sell from $30 to over $100, depending on the type and the number of stones. A variety of stones are available, including ones for serrated blades.

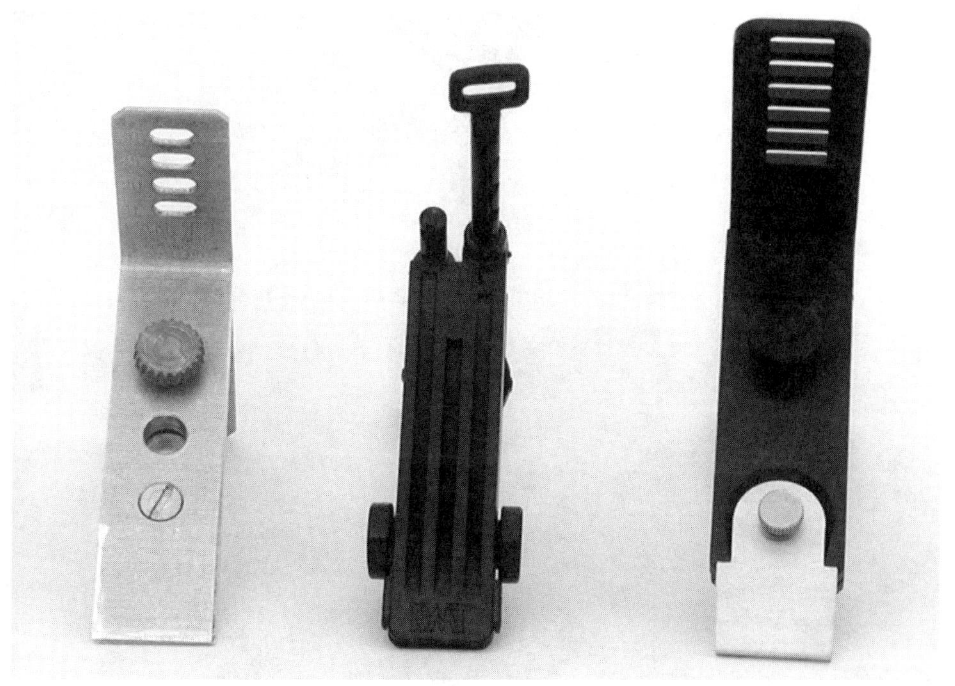

Rod-guided systems like these provide a selection of stones and angles.

The angles set by rod-guided systems aren't always what they are labeled and also can vary a lot from blade to blade. I found one well known guide to be off by 3 to 4 degrees from the indicated settings. This is not a problem as long as you are aware of it.

Most rod-guided systems will sharpen up to 4 inches of a long blade before you have to move the guide to a new position. One guide is designed so the blade is not clamped, which allows the entire blade to be sharpened as it is moved through the guide.

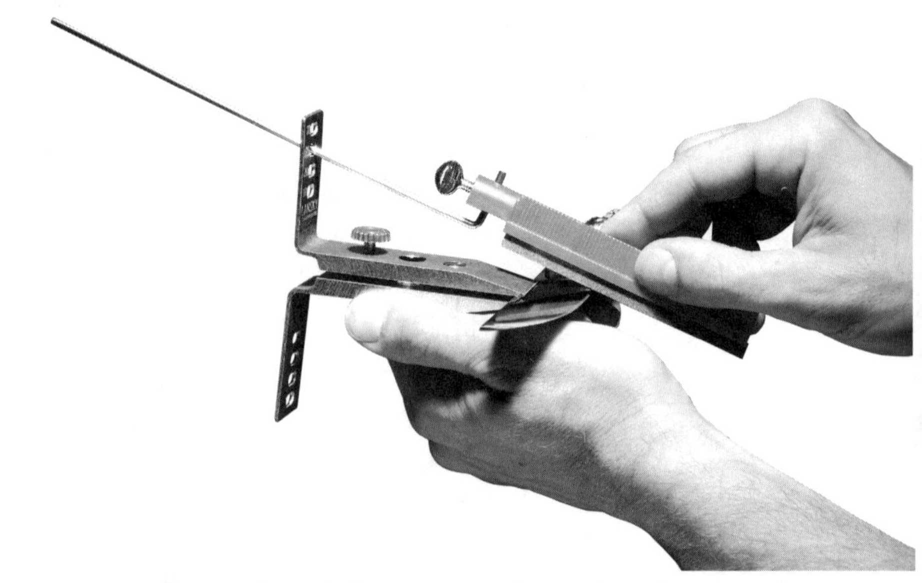

Lansky's rod-guided system can be used with the guide in one hand and the stone in the other.

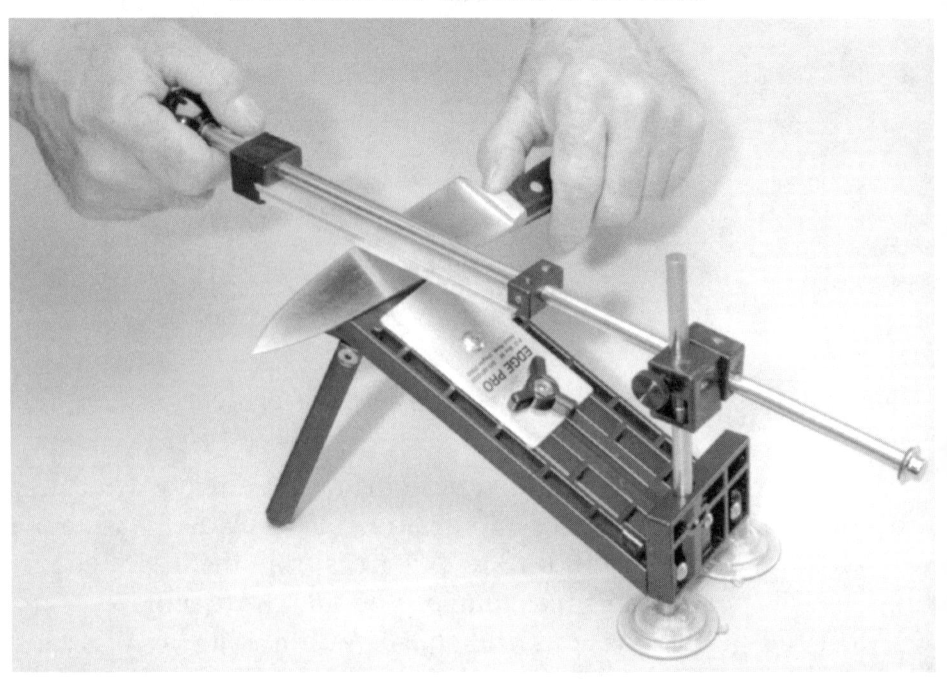

The EdgePro system is designed in such a manner that clamping the blade is unnecessary.

How to Sharpen a Knife

Sharpening Freehand

Sharpening freehand, that is, without a guide, is a familiar process so I won't go into it in much detail here. You have probably already done it, most likely with a double-sided bench stone. First you sharpen one side on the coarser stone until you raise a burr, or you feel you have sharpened enough, then you turn the blade over and sharpen an equal amount on the other side. The technique may use long sweeping strokes, back and forth, or circular strokes. Angle control starts as guesswork and becomes experience. When the burr is established, you turn the stone over to the fine side and remove it, generally with alternating strokes, continuing until you reach a satisfactory level of sharpness.

If you are successful with this method, good for you, you don't need to change anything. But if you haven't been successful, I want to introduce a method that is easy and foolproof.

Sharpening with a Guide

Sharpening with a guide is similar to the familiar manual sharpening method. The biggest change is the use of a guide. Some guides require a slightly different technique, and some even place the stones above the blade, but all are easy to learn to use. A novice using a guided system can produce as sharp an edge as the most experienced sharpener working freehand. The following instructions will work with either a guide for a bench stone or with a rod-guided system.

Select a knife that is not too dull, preferably one on which you can still see the original bevel. Start with a medium stone, about 300 to 360 grit. (If the blade is nicked or damaged or if you want to change the edge angle, you will need to begin with a coarse stone.)

Set up the guide according to the manufacturer's instructions and take a light stroke with the stone. Check the angle against the old bevel. If the new scratch pattern is on the back edge of the old bevel, the guide angle is set too low. If it is at the edge, the angle is set too high. When the scratch pattern is centered on the bevel you are duplicating the original angle. Keeping the original angle is a safe strategy to begin with.

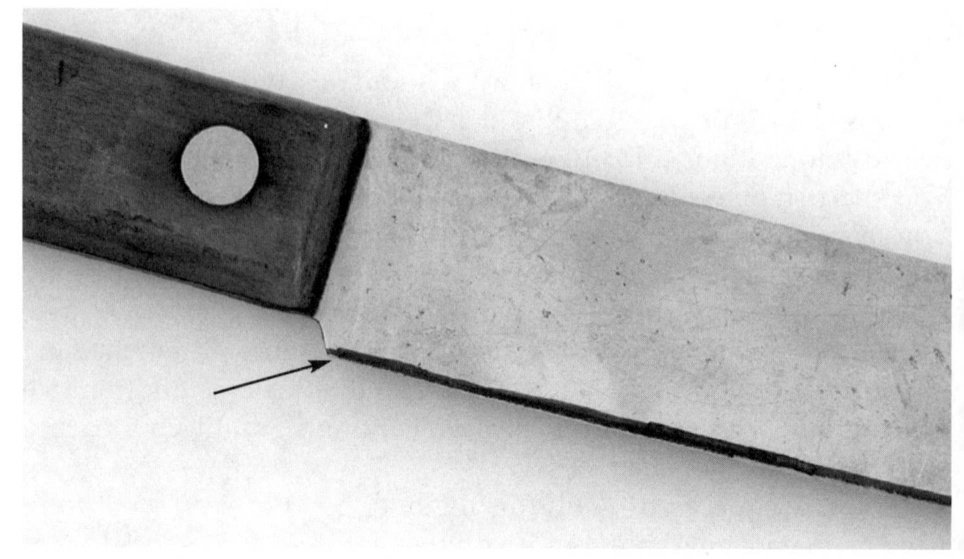

Marker is removed from the edge if the angle is greater than the original angle.

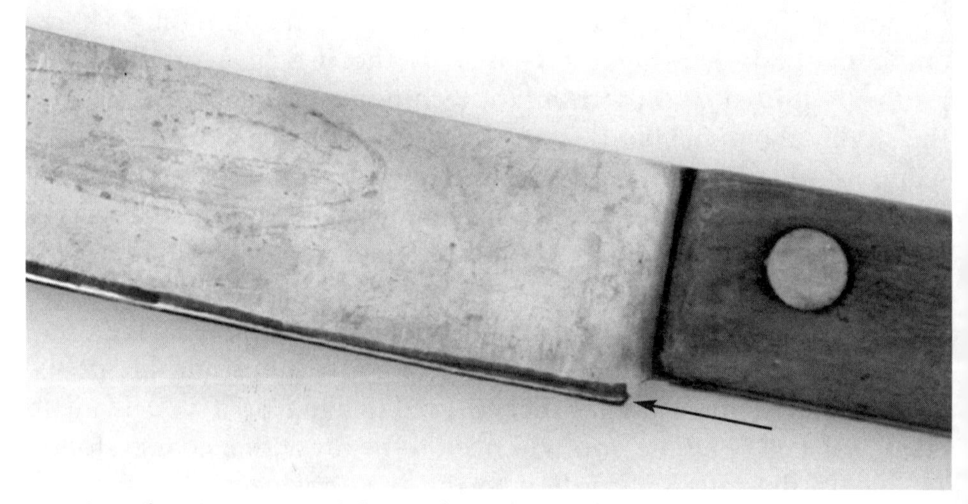

Marker is removed from the center of the bevel if the angle is the same as the original angle.

If you can't see the scratch pattern, try darkening the old bevel with a black felt tip marker, then stroke the stone again. The scratch pattern will stand out where it removes the dark marking.

NOTE: When using a sharpening guide near the tip, it should be positioned so that the distance from the tip to the pivot point is approximately equal to the distance from the edge to the pivot. This way the angle will be the same at the tip as at the edge, and will remain fairly constant around the curve approaching the tip. Do not let the guide or stone tilt when you get to the tip, or it will round it off.

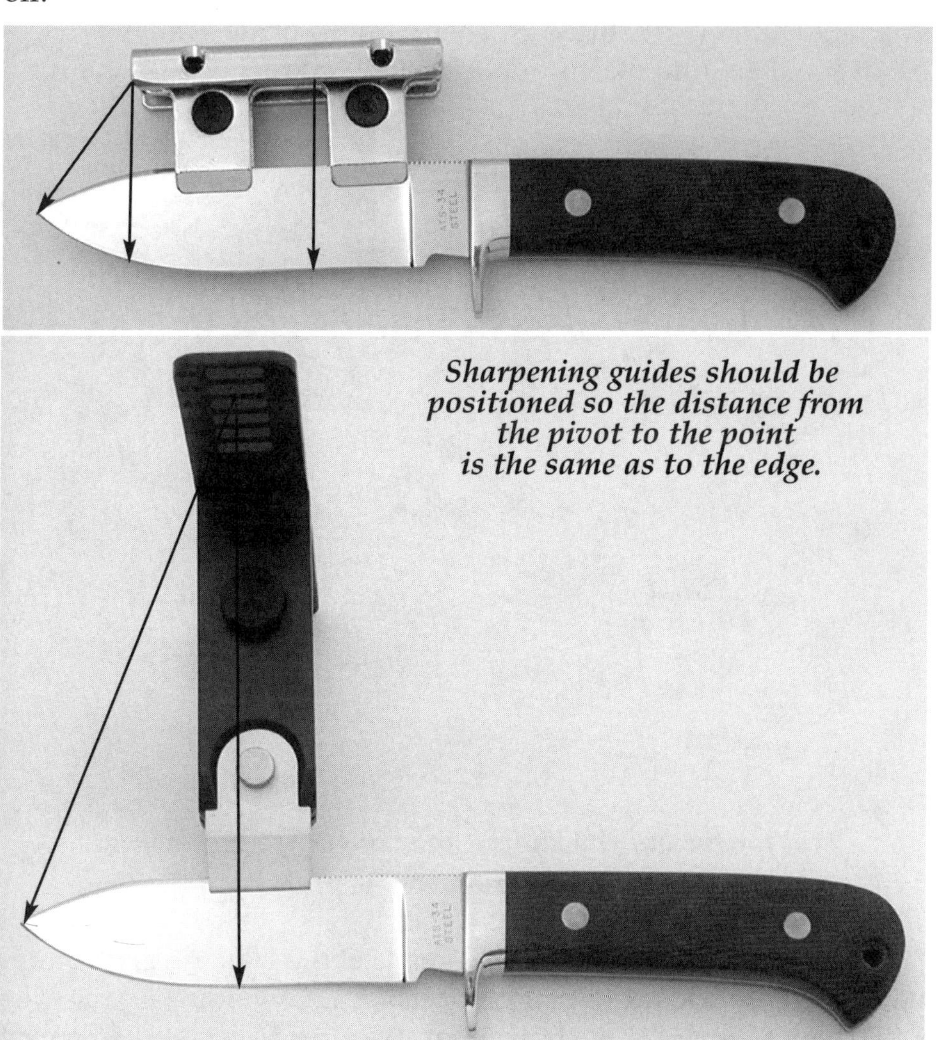

Sharpening guides should be positioned so the distance from the pivot to the point is the same as to the edge.

When the angle is set correctly, stroke one side of the blade until you have removed the old edge. There are several basic strokes – sliding the stone towards the edge, sliding it off the edge, or circular or alternating strokes. At the first stage, any of them is okay, but the stone produces a larger and easier to detect burr when sliding off the edge.

Sharpen on one side until you have raised a burr along the full length of the edge. The burr will appear on the side opposite the one you are sharpening. With experience you will learn how to stop with just a small burr in this step. If you are not sure, sharpen until you can definitely feel the burr. Then turn the blade over and sharpen an equal amount off the opposite side, producing a second burr.

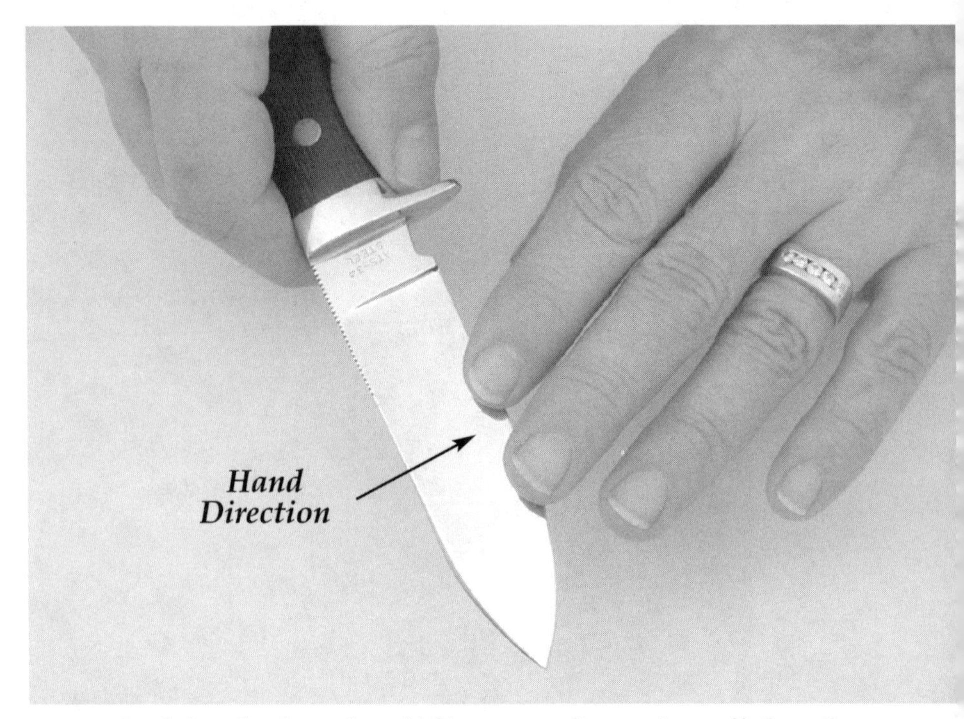

Feel for the burr by sliding your fingertips off the edge.

For the next step choose a fine stone, about 600 grit, and continue, using only strokes with the stone sliding towards the edge. The goal is not to remove much material. We already established a new edge when we created the burr. Now we just want to grind away the scratches made by the first stone. Alternate sides every few strokes. Finish with a few light strokes at a slightly higher angle, alternating sides, to remove the burr. This is where "slicing a decal off the stone" is an accurate description, because we want the edge and not the bevel against the stone.

Your edge should be reaching shaving sharpness. Test it as previously described. If there is roughness or the edge doesn't have enough bite, continue with the fine stone.

You may use the knife at this stage, as the edge will be sharp enough for most uses. It will shave hair from your arm or hand, but you wouldn't want to use it on your face. It now has 600 grit microserrations, which are sharp but wear and bend easily. Continue to the next step if you want a sharper, longer lasting edge.

Honing

You can further improve the edge by using an extra fine stone, 1000 grit or finer. Continue as above with this stone, maintaining the slightly greater angle that we established in the final step above. Continue with alternating strokes, about five to ten on each side. This is how we begin to create that polished secondary bevel that we saw on the razor blade.

Stropping

The final step to a mirror finish is to use a strop charged with a fine abrasive. This will improve the edge beyond where the finest stone or hone leaves off. The strop can be made of a variety of materials including cardboard and cloth, but I prefer leather glued to a wood block, split side up. An old-fashioned razor strop can also be used. Abrasives used can vary from valve lapping compound to jeweler's rouge. I prefer a green chromium oxide compound. Apply the compound sparingly, just enough to cover the whole strop without creating a build-up. Re-apply when the strop loses effectiveness. If a black glaze appears you are using too much compound. Remove it with a stiff brush and start over.

When stropping you *always* stroke off the edge to prevent cutting into the strop. Strop with strokes alternating from side to side until you obtain true razor sharpness. You're finished!

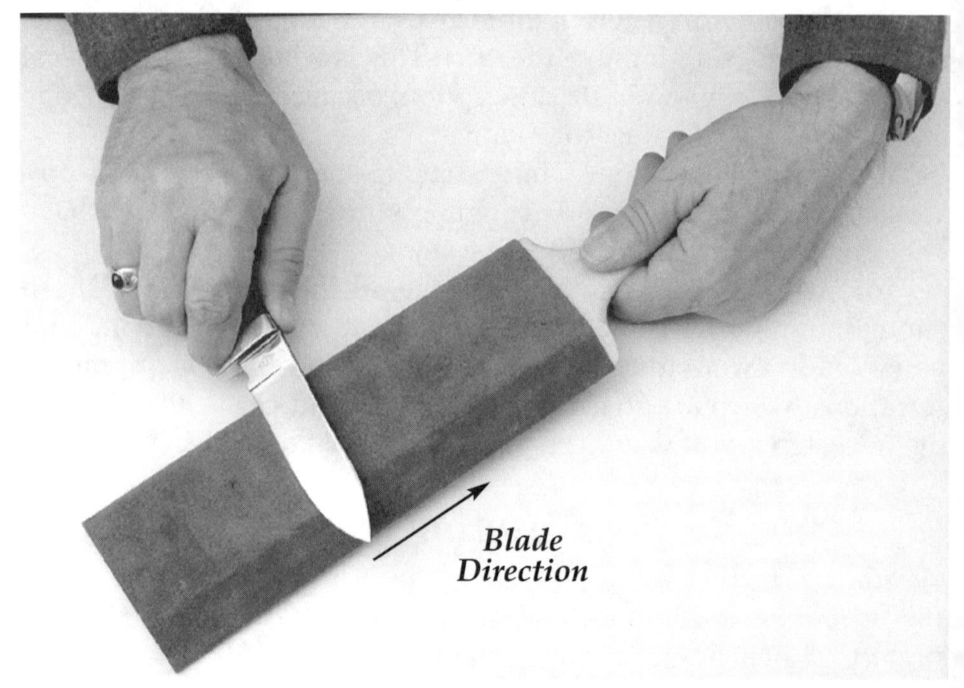

A few strokes on a strop will improve the edge better than the finest hone.

Using a Steel

A butcher's steel is essentially a round file with the teeth running the long way. They are intended for sharpening softer steel knives that are steeled several times a day, but are not suitable for today's tougher, harder steels. In my opinion, they belong in a museum along with natural stones.

The steel we want is smooth, and is called a meat packer's steel or a slick. It is a hardened, polished steel rod designed for straightening an edge. It is also useful for burnishing a newly finished edge. Smooth steels should be available wherever you buy knives.

The secret to using a steel is to use an angle about 10 degrees larger than the final honed edge. I am not aware of any guide for use with steels, but some do have a mark on the handle for the proper angle.

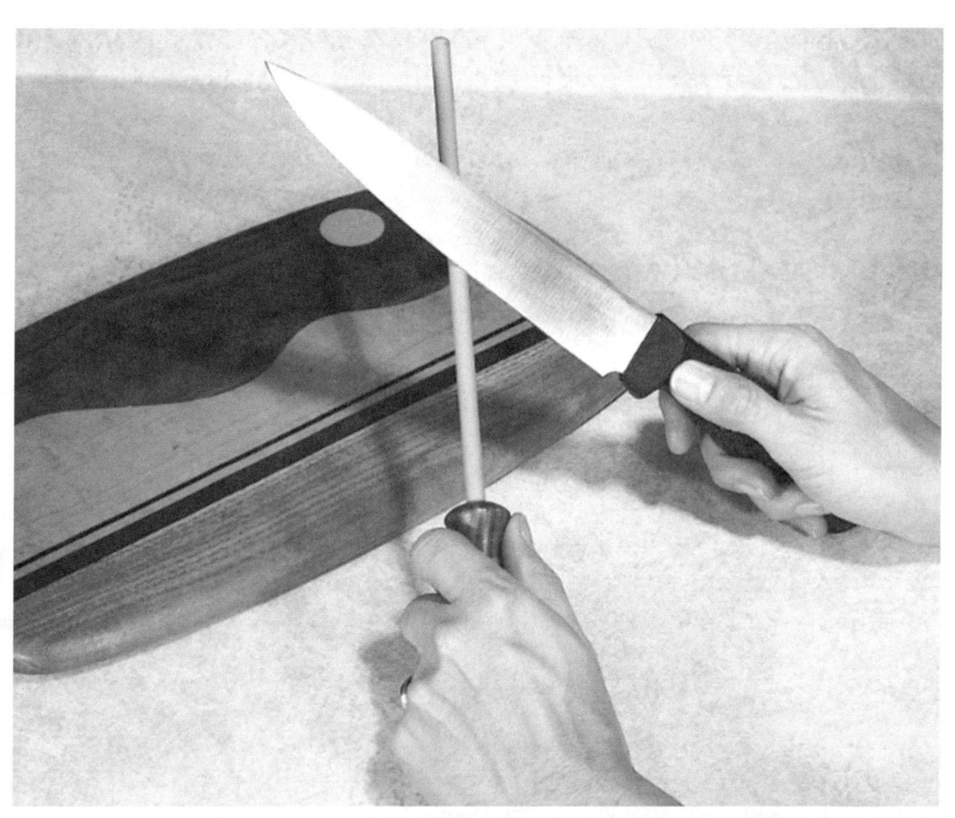

(Above)
The traditional method of steeling is to hold both the steel and the knife freehand.

(Right)
The preferred method of using a steel is to hold it vertical with the tip supported on a table.

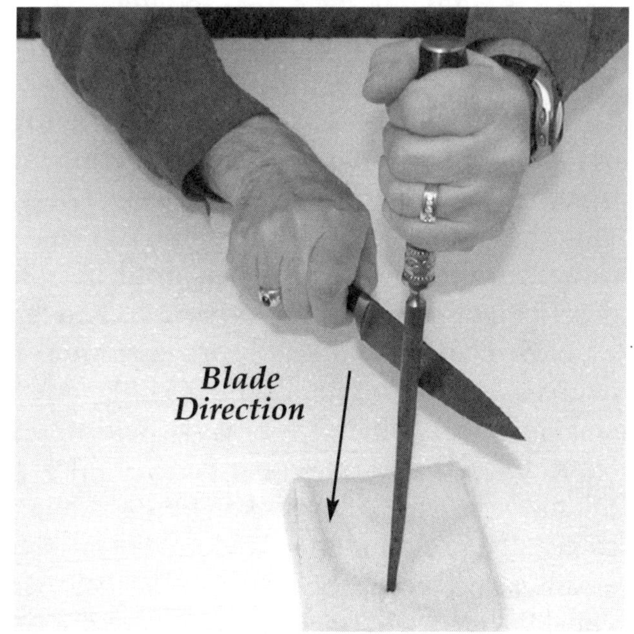

The best technique I have found is to hold the steel vertical with your weak hand, handle up and the tip pressed to a counter top or table (protect the counter or table with a towel or rag). Hold the knife in your strong hand and slice down the steel, alternating sides. Use light force. Because steels have a small diameter and they are pressing on a small edge, they exert high local pressure. This is how they affect the metal in a blade when used with very little force.

Steels rarely need maintenance, but if yours does, just polish it with crocus cloth.

A variation on the steel is the ceramic steel, where the steel rod is replaced by a ceramic one. Since ceramic is abrasive, it can polish as well as burnish. Ceramic steels are available from the same suppliers.

When the blade first becomes dull, a steel or fine touch-up stone will bring back the sharpness. When that no longer works, re-sharpen starting with the medium stone.

A Multi-Bevel Method

This variation will give you a longer lasting edge than the conventional method described above. The multi-bevel edge that results is similar to the convex edge popularly called a Moran edge. This method can be adapted to many types of sharpening equipment.

There are three steps. The first step is to establish an initial edge bevel about 4 or 5 degrees less than you want your final angle. This is sometimes referred to as pre-sharpening or thinning the blade. This step removes the most metal, but since you are using a coarse stone, it will go fast. Sharpen until the old edge is removed. As described above, the proof is that you have raised a burr.

Now change to a medium stone and set your guide for a few degrees' greater angle. By increasing the angle, we are grinding a smaller bevel, which saves work with the slower cutting medium stone. On a clamp-on type guide you increase the angle by moving the guide inward, closer to the edge. On a rod-guided system you can easily select another angle. Other systems have different ways to adjust the angle. See the section below for a method using the Lansky sharpener.

When you get to the fine stone, increase the angle again by another couple of degrees. Hone with strokes going towards the edge and alternate sides every few strokes. You are now working a very small area right at the edge, removing the burr and the scratches left by the medium stone.

Since each finer stone cuts more slowly, it takes quite a bit of work to remove the previous stone's scratches from the full bevel. By increasing the angle by a couple of degrees each time you change stones, you focus this work on a smaller area near the edge and reduce the work needed.

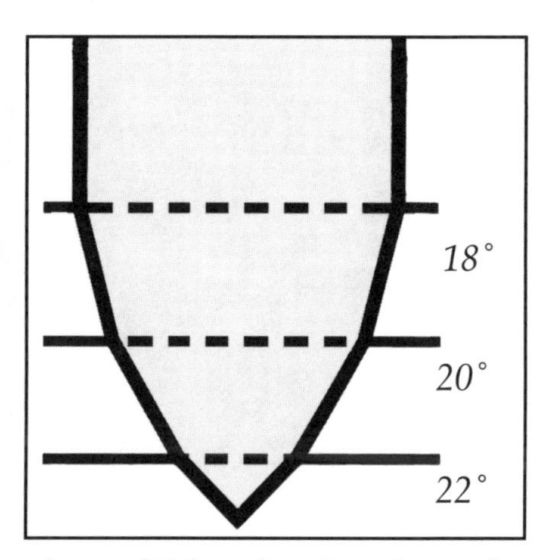

A multi-bevel edge has the advantages of a convex edge but can be made using guides.

Multi-bevel summary for a pocket knife:

Medium stone at 18 degrees,
Fine stone at 20 degrees,
Extra-fine stone at 22 degrees,
Strop.

Here is an easy way to do a multi-bevel with the Lansky rod-guided system:

Set the rod into the coarse stone as far as it will go and still have the screw tighten onto the flat. This decreases the angle by a degree or so. Set the extra-coarse stones the same if needed.

Set the rod on the medium stones per the instructions.

Set the rod into the fine stone only far enough to tighten the screw onto the flat. This increases the angle by a degree or so. Set the extra-fine the same if you have one.

Now, when using these stones you will automatically create a three-bevel edge without changing the guide.

TIP: Replacing the thumb screws on a Lansky rod-guided system with flat head screws will give you another half inch or so of useful stone travel, as the thumb screws impede the stone's movement.

Special Cases and Advanced Techniques

Daggers and Double-Edged Blades

It is difficult to clamp a double-edged blade in a guide so that the centerline is the properly aligned. The best that can be done is to clamp the blade using one of the blade's flat surfaces as a reference surface, and adjust the sharpening angle to match the original angle. Since these are often used for stabbing cuts, pay attention to the point as described below.

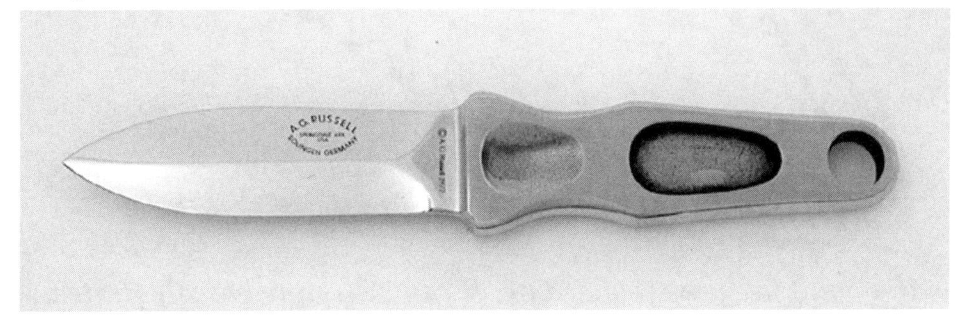

Double edged knives require special attention.

Maintaining the Point

The point of a knife blade consists of three or more surfaces coming together. (Three for a single-edged blade, four for a dagger or double-edged blade.) To prevent the point from becoming rounded, use flat stones and avoid sharpening with too much pressure on the point. Using flexible abrasives or crock sticks will round off the point.

When the point does become rounded off or broken, grinding the back side of the blade – the third surface – can restore it. Also, prolonged sharpening of a folding knife blade can cause the point to rise relative to the rest of the blade, so that it may no longer be enclosed when the knife is closed. Grinding down the back side will also correct this.

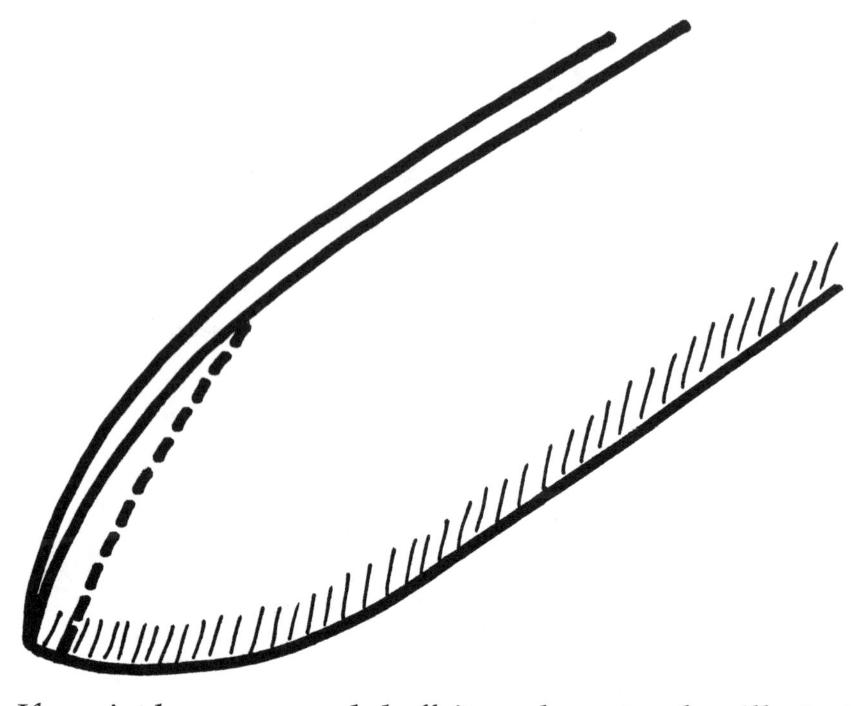

If a point becomes rounded off, it can be restored as illustrated.

Recurved Blades

A recurved or hawksbill blade is not difficult to sharpen. It is just that the concave edge of a recurved blade cannot be sharpened with a flat stone. A stone that is curved or round in cross-section is needed, with a radius equal or smaller than the blade curve. A crock stick or a ceramic steel works well for these blades. If you have a rod-guided system with a stone for serrated blades, it can also be used. Otherwise, you will have to sharpen without a guide.

With that in mind, simply sharpen by hand following the steps outlined for standard blade shapes: stay close to the original edge angle, raise a burr on one side, sharpen an equal amount on the other side, then remove the burr and polish the edge with finer stones.

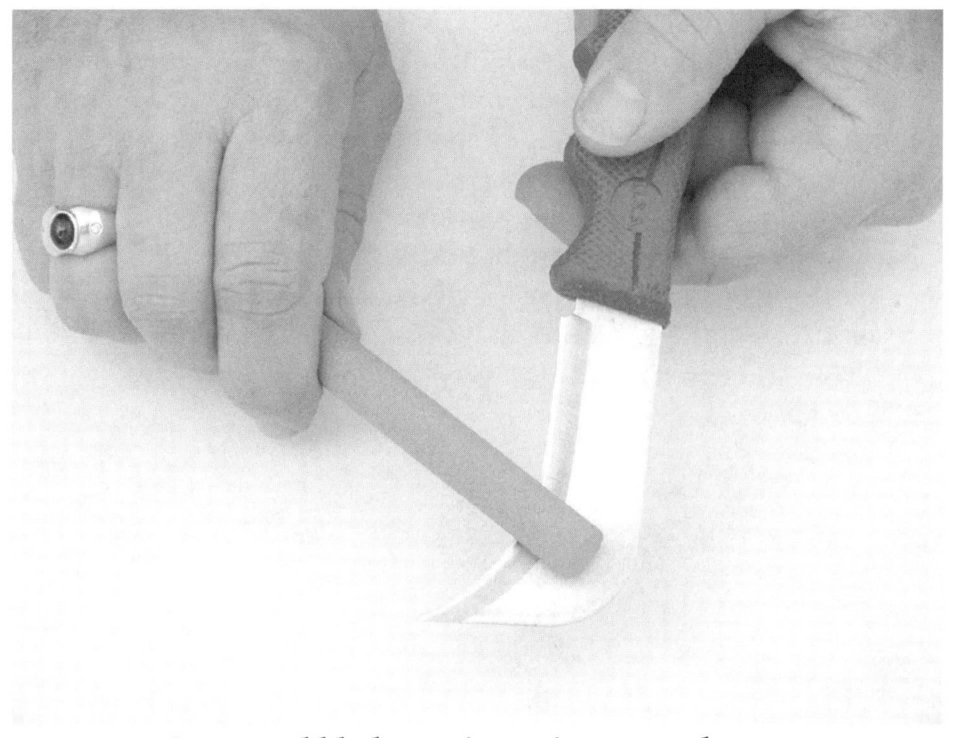

A recurved blade requires using a round stone smaller than the blade radius.

Serrated Blades

In addition to style, there are two main reasons to consider a knife with a serrated blade. First, the serrations cut with varying angles of attack - front, back and top - which is very beneficial in cutting fibrous material like rope or meat. Second, the projecting parts of the serrations protect the sharp recessed edges from damage caused by hitting the cutting board or plate.

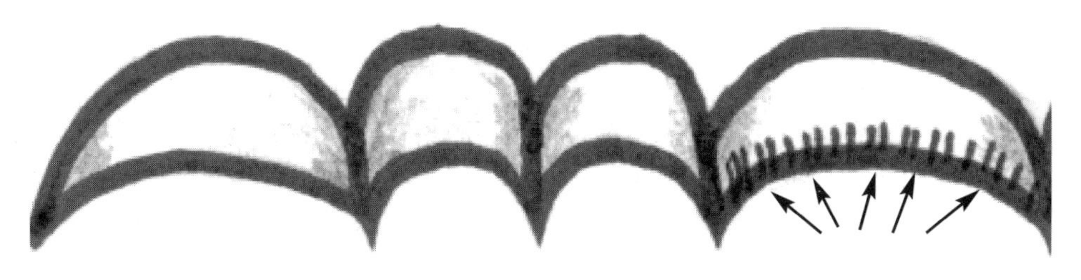

Serrations cut material from several different angles.

My advice on serrated knives is to buy them from a manufacturer who offers lifetime resharpening. There are many serration patterns on the market, often patented or trademarked by the manufacturer. Most are too small and/or complicated to be sharpened easily at home without a special sharpener.

If you insist on sharpening your own, Spyderco and Lansky offer special stones with the right profile for serrated blades. The triangular rods of the Spyderco SharpMaker will fit some but not all serrations. A simple scalloped edge, not more than four serrations per inch, can be fairly easily resharpened with a simple rod sharpener.

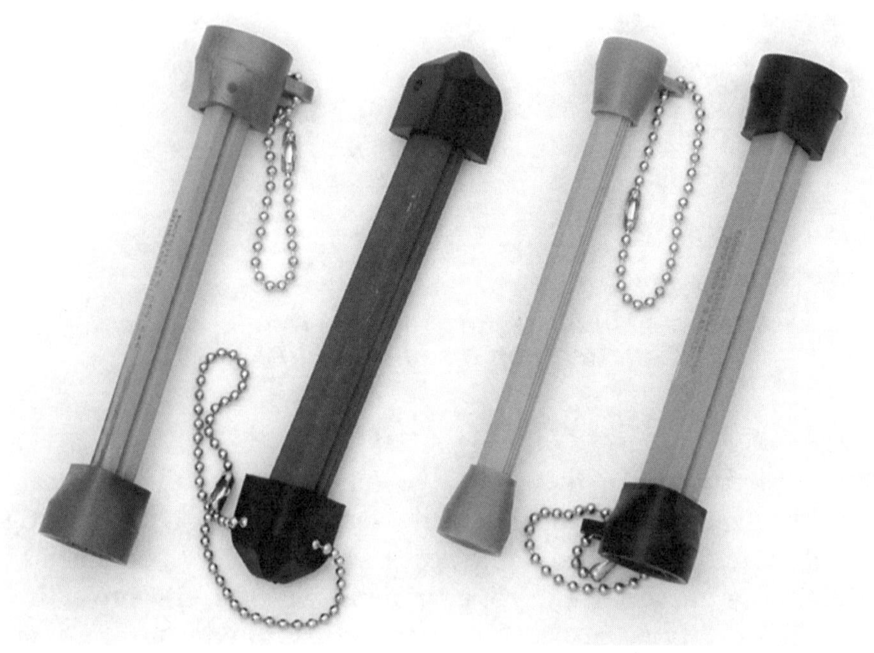

Spyderco and Lansky make stones for different types of serrated blades.

Serrated edges are ground from only one side, creating a single bevel edge. When new they may still have a burr from manufacturing, usually on the back or flat side. Remove this burr with a fine flat stone, honing either flat or with just a few degrees of angle. One way to maintain a very small angle is to place masking tape on the back near the spine of the blade and let the tape act as a guide. This will also protect the blade's finish at the same time.

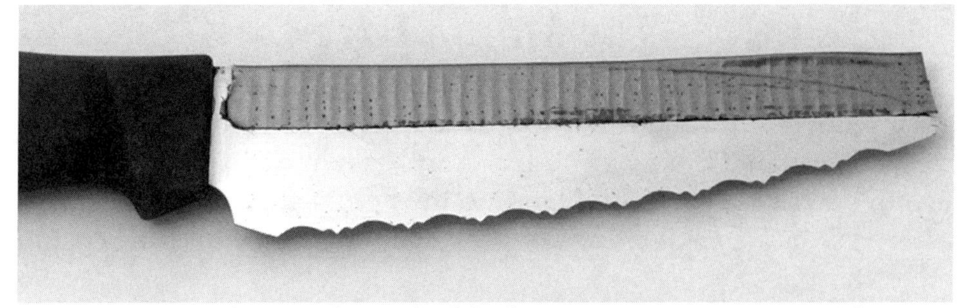

A strip of tape along the blade's spine serves as a guide when removing the burr.

Next, polish each serration with a ceramic rod. Check from front to back and see if the burr is moving back and forth, and keep honing until it is removed.

Finally, you can use your regular stone and guide to sharpen the points between the serrations. This will give the edge the initial penetrating ability that is needed to cut delicate fruits like ripe tomatoes. This step can be used on any style of serrated blade except a steak knife. The main purpose of serration points on a steak knife is to protect the plate. They should be blunt for this reason.

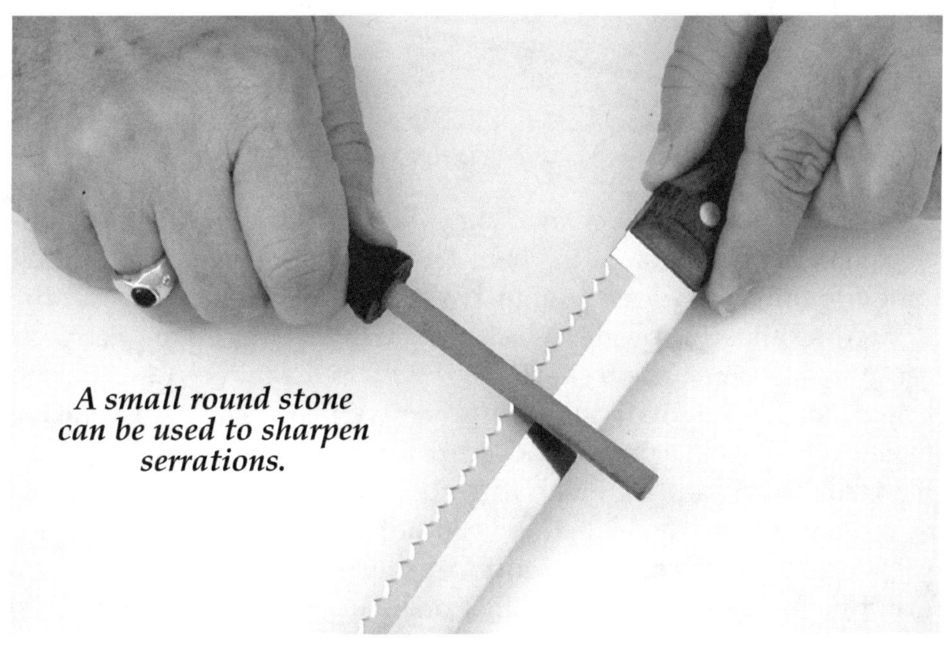

A small round stone can be used to sharpen serrations.

The Moran Edge

The convex edge, popularized by maker Bill Moran, is an edge with many names. The shape is technically a cannel, and therefore the proper name is a cannel edge. Another name is the "appleseed" grind, because of its resemblance to the pointy end of an appleseed. This edge has the advantage of greater strength at very little cost in edge sharpness.

Light sharpening of a convex edge can be done with a guide and a fine stone just like a regular beveled edge. They can also be sharpened by hand, because our natural tendency to round the bevel is compatible with a convex edge. But eventually we will need to do a full sharpening to restore the convex shape and appearance.

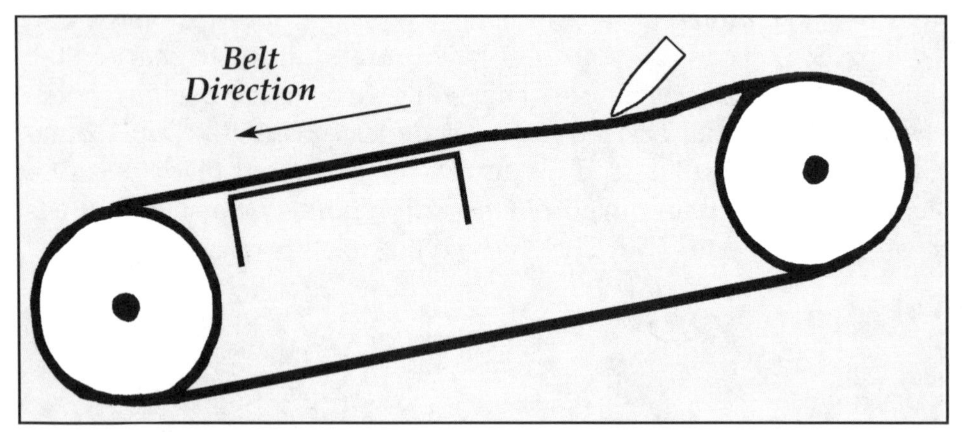

The slack portion of a belt grinder produces a convex edge.

The convex edge is created on a belt grinder using an unsupported or slack section of the belt. These grinders are similar to belt sanders, but with special contact wheels and platens to grind the desired profiles, including a slack section for convex edges. See p. 81 for more information on sharpening with belt sanders.To duplicate this condition for sharpening at home we need a flexible abrasive like silicon carbide paper, backed up with a flexible backing like foam rubber. A sanding block with sponge rubber backing available at the hardware store fills this need admirably. Use the same progression of grit sizes as conventional sharpening – medium or 300 grit, fine or 600 grit, and extra fine or 1000 grit.

When using any flexible or soft abrasive, it is important to limit our sharpening strokes to those moving the abrasive off the edge. This will prevent the edge from cutting into the abrasive.

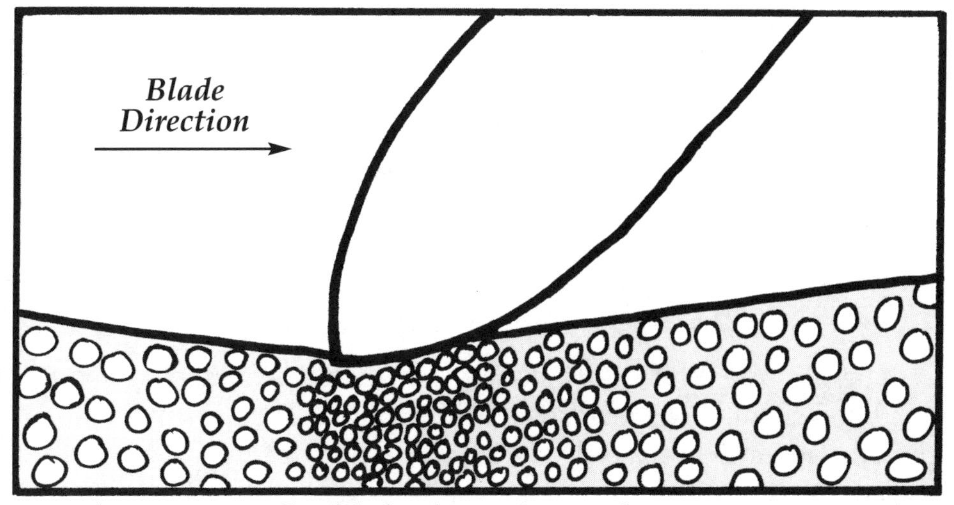

An abrasive on a flexible backing also conforms to a convex edge.

The Chisel Edge

The chisel or single bevel blade is becoming popular. Custom makers like their unique appearance, and manufacturers find they are inexpensive to grind. There are still two surfaces coming together to form the edge, the angles have just changed. The back has no bevel, or zero degrees. The chisel bevel is angled greater than on a double bevel blade, usually 30 degrees or so. If an extra 10 degrees is used for the final sharpening angle, the total 40-degree angle is the same as a double bevel blade with 20-degree bevels.

People used to a double bevel will have trouble cutting straight with a chisel edge at

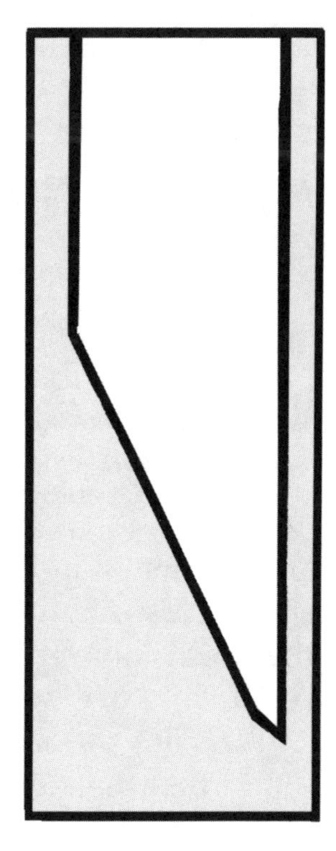

The chisel edge has only a single bevel and is sharpened on only one side.

first. However, once you are used to it, the flat side actually makes it easier to cut straight.

To get good sharpness, the back needs to be flat and polished smooth. This is easily done by simply laying the blade flat on the stone. No guide is needed. If you want to protect the backside finish, you can hone it at a very low angle, using tape along the spine to protect it like we did for the serrated blade (pp. 52-53).

The edge bevel is sharpened next, using our guide. Hone the back again to remove the sharpening burr. Most of the guides for bench stones will not allow the 30 to 40 degree angles needed here. Most rod-guided systems will.

The Japanese Sashimi Knife

The sashimi knife is typical of Asian knives. Its single bevel helps the sushi chef make straight thin slices. They are available in right hand and left hand models. The big difference between a sashimi knife and a chisel edge knife is that the sashimi knife is intended to be sharpened on the back side. The back side is hollow ground to make this easier.

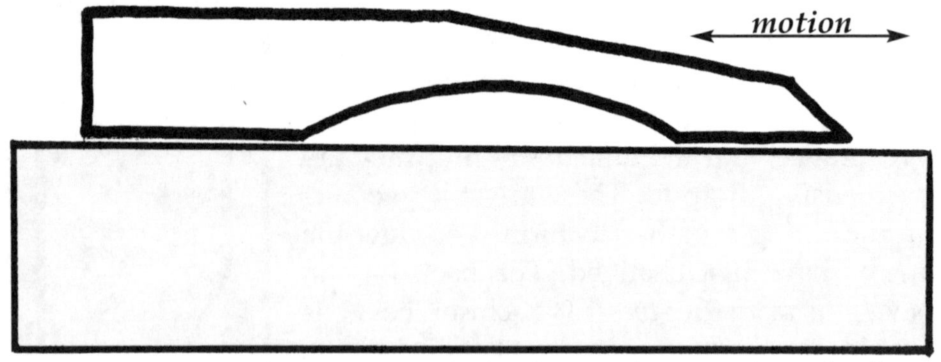

The sashimi knife has a chisel edge but is sharpened on the flat side, which is hollow ground to make this easier.

The first step is to make sure the front bevel is polished and smooth. Use a guide and treat this bevel just like a regular knife. If the edge is nicked, sharpening this edge is the way to fix it. Finally, polish this bevel with your finest stone.

Next, lay the back of the blade flat on the stone and push it edge first across the stone, pressing down with your fingertips. Repeat until sharp. Usually only 5 to 10 strokes are needed.

The traditional choice of stones for sashimi knives is Japanese waterstones, and it is an excellent choice. They cut fast, and the 8000 grit "gold" waterstone contains the finest abrasive available in a stone form. People who use it never need to move to stropping or polishing to achieve razor sharpness.

Ceramic Knives

Ceramic knives are becoming more popular, and are very good knives for slicing vegetables. Most of them come with a lifetime sharpening warranty, but you may wish to try sharpening them yourself. Since these knives hold an edge so well, they will only need honing with an extra-fine abrasive and stropping. There are two basic types of ceramic blades, white ones made of zirconium oxide (zirconia) and black ones made of zirconium carbide.

Two from Boker's line of ceramic kitchen knives.

Diamond hones can sharpen a ceramic knife, but you must use fine hones and remove all scratches caused by the diamonds. Never use a coarse hone. Scratches concentrate the stress and can cause the brittle ceramic blade to fracture.

Silicon carbide wheels or stones can be used to sharpen ceramic knives, which are made of relatively softer aluminum oxide. Since paper wheels use silicon carbide abrasive, they too can sharpen ceramic knives. Silicon carbide wheels can also remove the scratches from sharpening with diamonds.

Ceramic blades will not raise a burr. You'll have to go directly to other tests to determine when a ceramic knife is sharp.

Beyond Knives

Sharpening Straight Razors

Until the invention of the safety razor, every man who shaved learned to sharpen his straight razor. Today, most of us have never needed to learn. Fortunately, the razor is designed to make sharpening easy. The straight razor features a double-sided, hollow ground blade, with the thickness of the spine such that it acts as a sharpening guide. No other guide is needed.

The straight razor is hollow ground on both sides to make sharpening easy.

A straight razor should be stropped before each shave. An image we have of the straight razor is our barber slapping it on the strop hanging from the side of the barber chair just before putting the final touches on our haircut. This strop has two sides, one of coarse canvas, whose purpose is straightening any burr on the edge, and one of leather to give the edge a final polishing. There is enough natural abrasiveness in the leather that it never has to be charged with stropping compound. As with any flexible abrasive, the blade is always pulled backwards, with the strop sliding off the razor's edge.

Periodically, the razor will need to be honed in order to reestablish the edge bevel. Hones for razors are made with very fine abrasives. Although they look like black Arkansas stones, they are man-made, and often have the maker's name molded into them. To hone a straight razor, treat each side of the razor just like the back side of the sashimi knife (p. 56), laying it flat on the hone and pushing it across edge first. The razor will need to be stropped before use as described above.

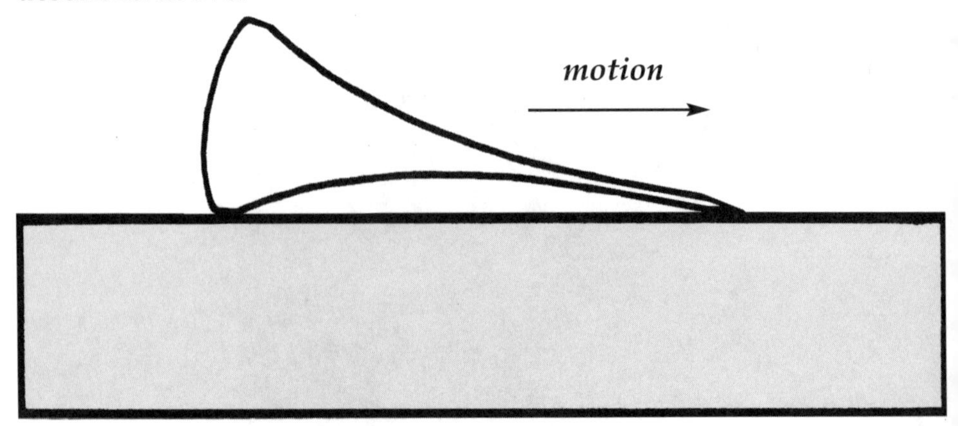

The thick spine of the straight razor serves as its guide.

Sharpening Vegetable Peelers

The household vegetable peeler can be improved with sharpening. It has two edges facing each other. Normally, one is used to cut and the other acts as a guide that determines the thickness of the peeling. First, determine which is the cutting edge depending on how you use the peeler. If your peeler has two users with different techniques, I suggest getting two peelers. It is difficult to get both edges to perform well on the same peeler.

Lay the peeler on the bench so that the cutting edge is nearest you. Use a small stone to sharpen the cutting edge, following the original bevel. Next, slide a small round stone back and forth inside the peeler to remove the burr. A small ceramic rod works well.

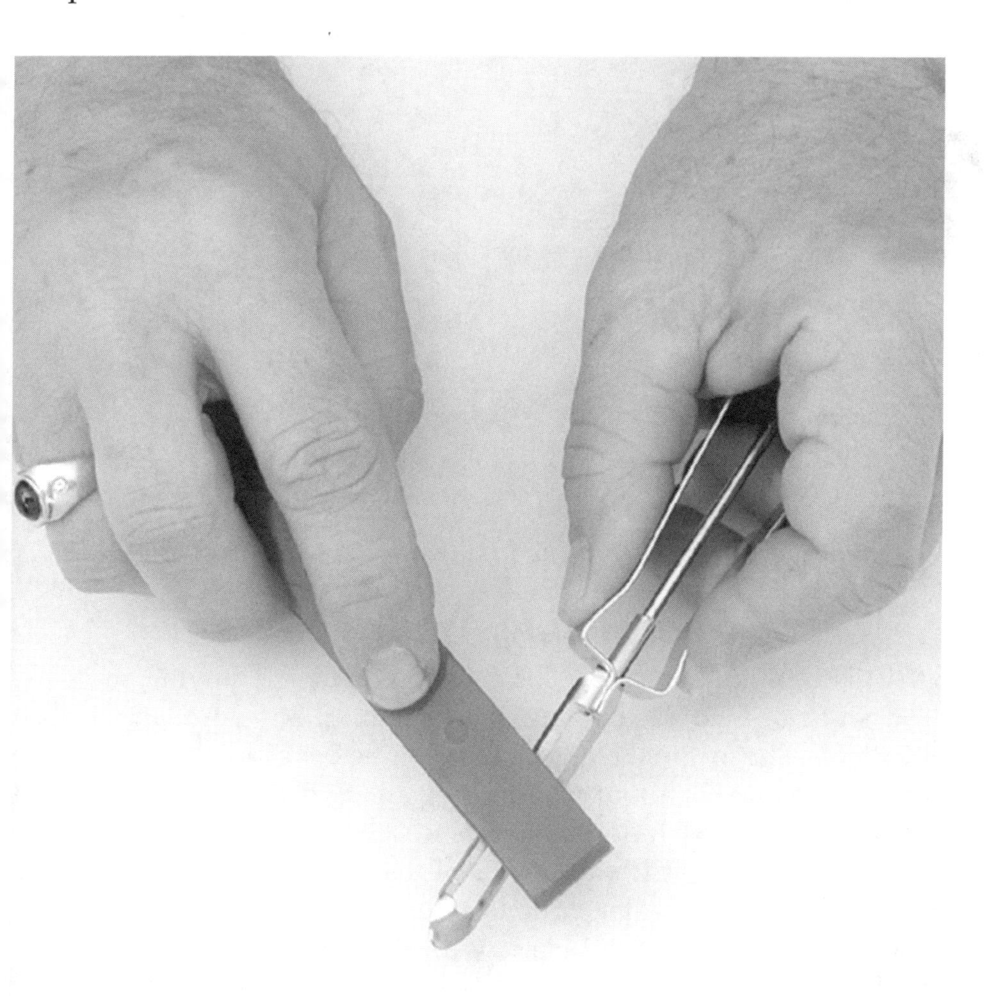

The household vegetable peeler can be sharpened with a small stone.

If you have a finer small stone, use it to put on a secondary bevel, then use it inside to hone off any burr. Some stones made for serrated blades have one round corner that is useful here.

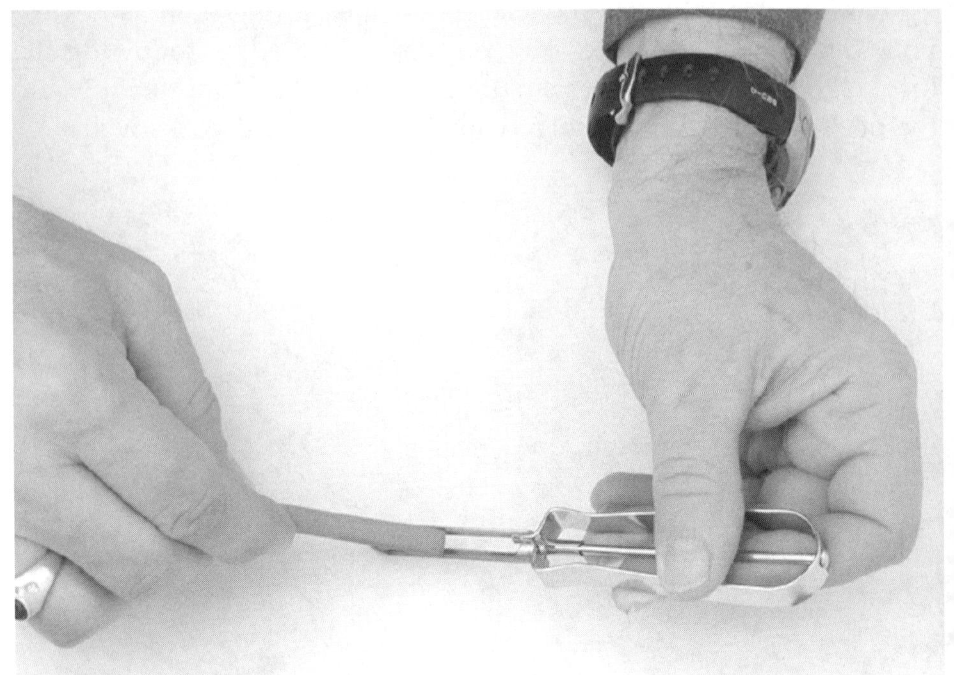

Remove the burr from the inside with a small round stone.

Sharpening Apple Corers

This tool cuts an apple into sections while removing the core. You will not be able to sharpen everything, but you can sharpen most of it. The original blades have a single bevel, but are so dull we will break our rule about maintaining an edge's original bevels and resharpen them with double bevels.

A tungsten carbide slot device of the type you grip like a pistol so the cutters are under your thumb is the best sharpener to use now. Sharpen each radial blade with it. You will need to alternate strokes inside out, then outside in, to reach into the corners. Repeat until light no longer reflects off the edges. Touch up with a small stone, and then sharpen the center blade with a conical grinding stone mounted in a drill or drill press.

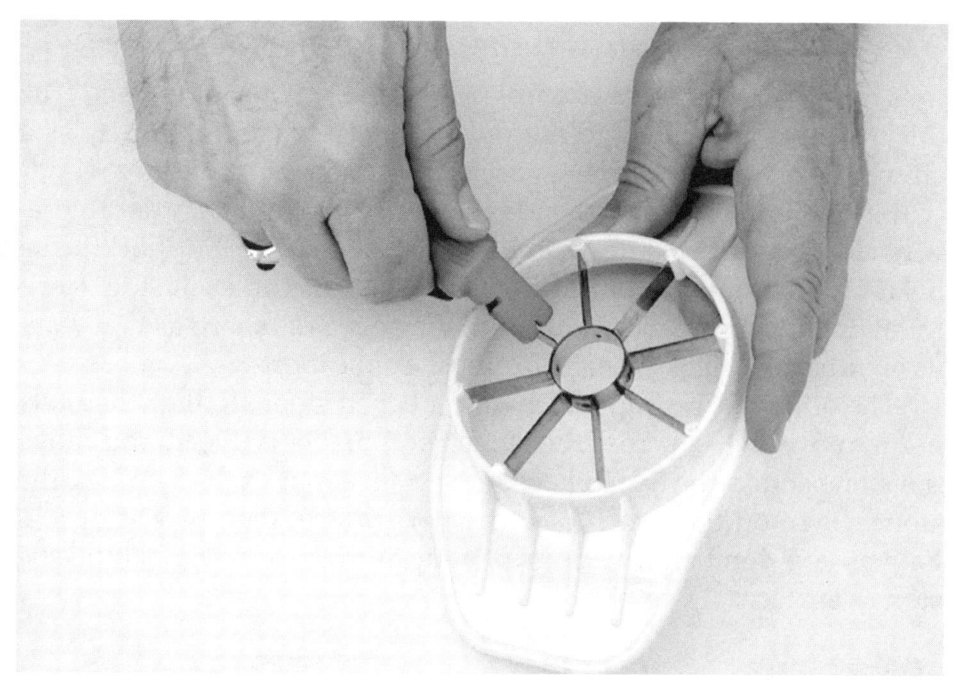

The radial blades of an apple corer can be sharpened with a tungsten carbide sharpener, then touched up with a small stone.

The center blade can be sharpened with a 1-inch conical grinding stone mounted in a drill or drill press.

Sharpening Axes

The ax is the ultimate example of the convex or Moran edge. The thickness behind the edge not only gives it strength, but acts as a chip breaker when chopping and as a wedge when splitting wood.

Since the steel in an ax head is softer than a knife in order to prevent chipping, sharpening can be started with a file. Support the ax head on a workbench or cutting block, and file on each side. Keep following the original contour until the edge is as sharp as you want it. File sharpening is enough for most applications.

The edge can be improved with a bench stone. Rather than trying to move the ax across the stone, support the ax head and move the stone across the ax. To keep your fingers out of the way, lay the stone down on the bench or other flat surface, then pick it up. As long as you don't shift your grip, your fingers are safely behind the stone's surface.

An ax can be sharpened with a file or a bench stone.

Special round stones are made just for axes and other outdoor tools.

A circular stroke is easiest to use when sharpening an ax. A coarse stone is probably all you will need, but you can keep on with finer stones until you can shave with it. If you have a belt grinder, the slack belt technique discussed previously also works well with an ax (p. 54).

Sharpening Swords and Machetes

If the blade is very large, it helps to lay the blade on the edge of a workbench with the edge exposed, and move the stone over the edge as we did with the ax. Lay the stone down on the bench then pick it up like we did for the ax. This will assure that your fingers are above the stone's surface and away from the edge. If your grip moves, lay the stone down and pick it up again so you don't expose a fingertip.

Sharpening Chisels

Like its namesake the chisel edge knife, the chisel features a single bevel edge. The big difference is that the edge is at the end of the tool instead of being on the side. Guides for sharpening chisels and plane irons are designed for use with bench stones.

Flatten the back side of the chisel first, using flat stones or wet-or-dry sandpaper on a flat plate such as a piece of glass. A few drops of water will hold the paper in place if you don't want to glue it down. The finished back should have a mirror finish, at least at the edge. Waterstones or automotive finishing sandpaper can polish this fine, or you can use a strop. Be careful using a strop or flexible abrasive on the back or it will round off the edge. This is very important with woodworking tools, where the edge geometry plays an important role in cutting. Don't worry about getting the entire back polished, this can develop with future sharpenings.

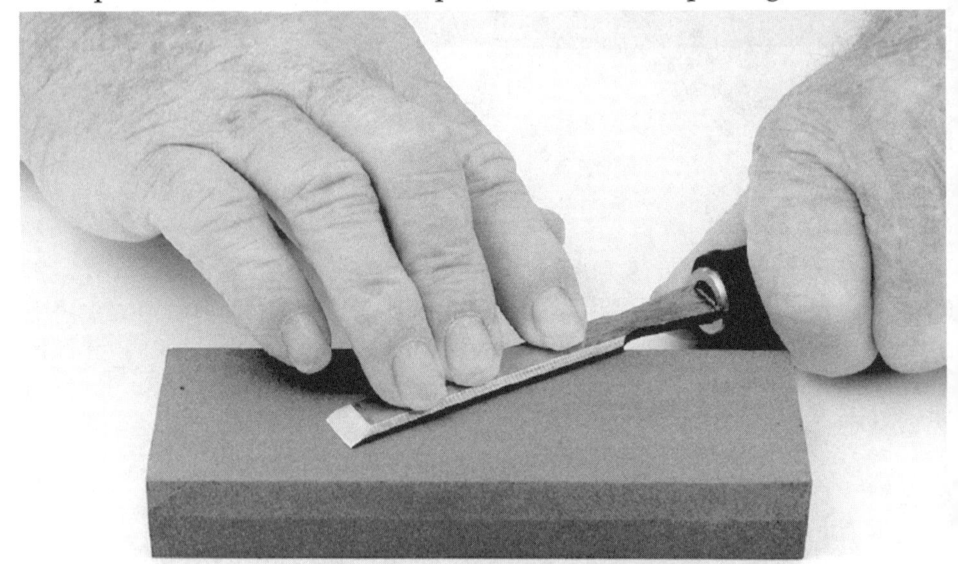

Flattening the back of a chisel.

Next, sharpen the bevel on a medium stone until a burr develops. This angle is usually 30 degrees, but if you have the time and the inclination, 25 degrees is better and will reduce future sharpening time.

Now increase the guide angle to the desired cutting angle, usually 35 degrees. One chisel and plane iron guide has this angle increase built in; all you have to do is turn a knob. Move to a fine stone and add the secondary bevel. This will remove or at least reduce the burr. Finally, flatten the back again briefly to remove any remaining burr.

Sharpening Plane Irons

The blade of a plane, called an iron, is a wide chisel designed to fit in the plane, which acts to control the cut. When you remove the iron from a plane, notice whether the bevel is up or down. The most common amateur mistake is putting the iron back in the wrong position. Bench planes have the bevel down; block planes have the bevel up.

A plane iron is sharpened similarly to a chisel. The steps are:
Flatten the back with a fine stone,
Sharpen the primary bevel with a medium stone,
Sharpen the secondary bevel with a fine stone,
Flatten the back again with the fine stone, removing any burr.

A plane iron's edge should have a small curvature so that the corners do not leave marks. This is accomplished by applying pressure to the corners in steps 2 and 3.

If a chisel or plane iron is badly damaged, it helps to grind the damaged area away and square the tip before sharpening. A burr across this straight new surface assures us that the edge is not skewed.

These guides are for plane irons and chisels. The guide on the right will also hold knives.

Sharpening Scissors and Shears

Some knife sharpeners can sharpen scissors and are adequate for everyday scissors and shears. Scissors used for barbering and dress-making should be professionally sharpened.

Most scissors and shears consist of two nearly identical blades, each having a single bevel sharpened at 60 to 80 degrees. Because they meet each other, it is important that scissor blades be sharpened carefully. Rounding of the edge causes the blades to pinch off the material rather than cut it, and a burr on either edge can make the blades cut into each other and cause early failure.

If possible, disassemble the two blades and sharpen them individually. Begin sharpening by setting up your system to match the original bevel angle. Carefully sharpen each blade with a medium stone until any rounding, visible as a glint, is removed. If you are not able to separate the two blades, be very careful not to hit the other blade with the stone and ruin its edge.

You do not polish this edge or make a secondary bevel as we did with knives. It is desirable for this bevel to remain somewhat rough, which prevents the material from slipping as the blade closes. Some scissors and shears have one of these bevels serrated. If you want to sharpen this, you'll need a checkering file. These are available from gunsmith and knifemaker supply houses.

Before we close the scissors for the first time, we need to remove the burr by honing the flat inside surface of each blade. Lay the blade flat on a very fine stone and hone lightly, being careful not to rock the blade. Another method is to burnish the burr up over the bevel by using a smooth steel flat on the inside surface. Separate the blades before closing them the first time, then close them without letting them touch. This will make sure the blades are not cutting into each other.

Finally, adjust the pivot screw so that the two blades meet for their full length with enough pressure to cut well without cutting into each other. A little experimentation may be needed.

With pruning shears, one blade is an anvil or hook designed to hold the material being cut, and the cutting blade is sharpened like a chisel at about 30 degrees.

Other Sharpening Equipment

Ceramic Rods

I have already mentioned the ceramic sharpening steel which is used just like a regular steel. Another type of ceramic rod sharpener is called a "crock stick." Operation is completely different than with bench stones or rod-guided systems. Two sticks are held in an upright vee at a predetermined angle, and the blade is brought down against them in a slicing motion. This is an excellent, easy to use system that has won lots of converts. You can make deviations from the set angle by tilting the blade.

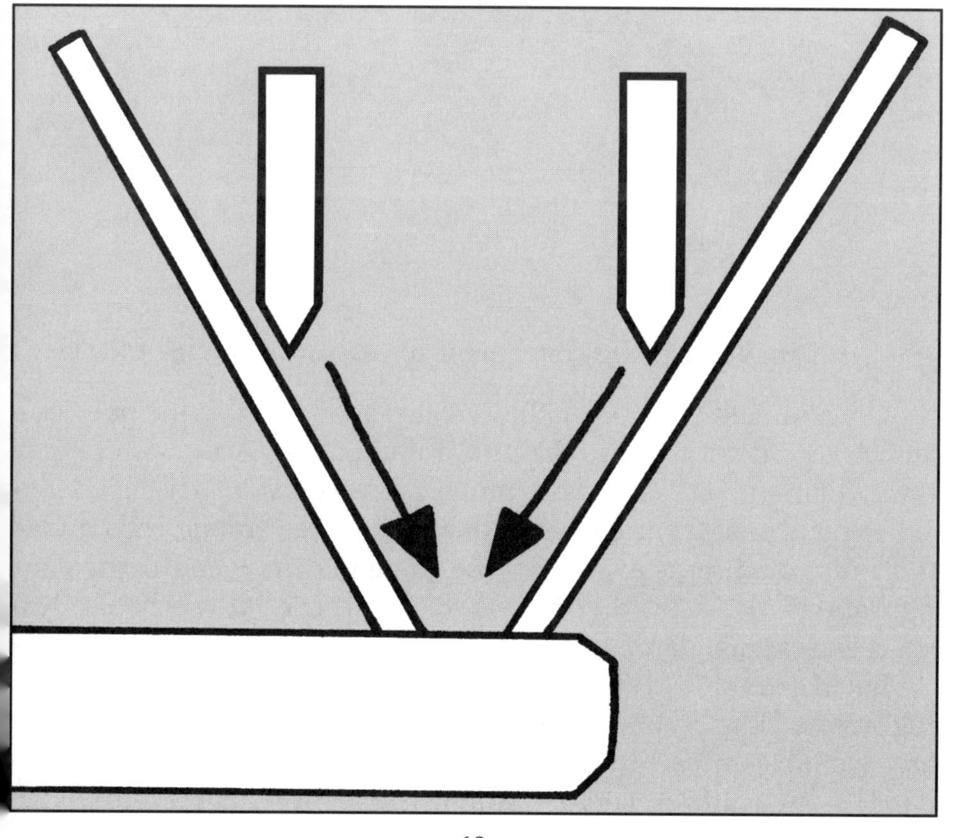

One minor problem with ceramic rods is that they round off the point of the blade as it is drawn across them. If you like a really sharp point, the best way to sharpen them is with a flat stone.

One ceramic rod sharpener folds for easy carrying. It is handy for sharpening fillet and hunting knives in the field.

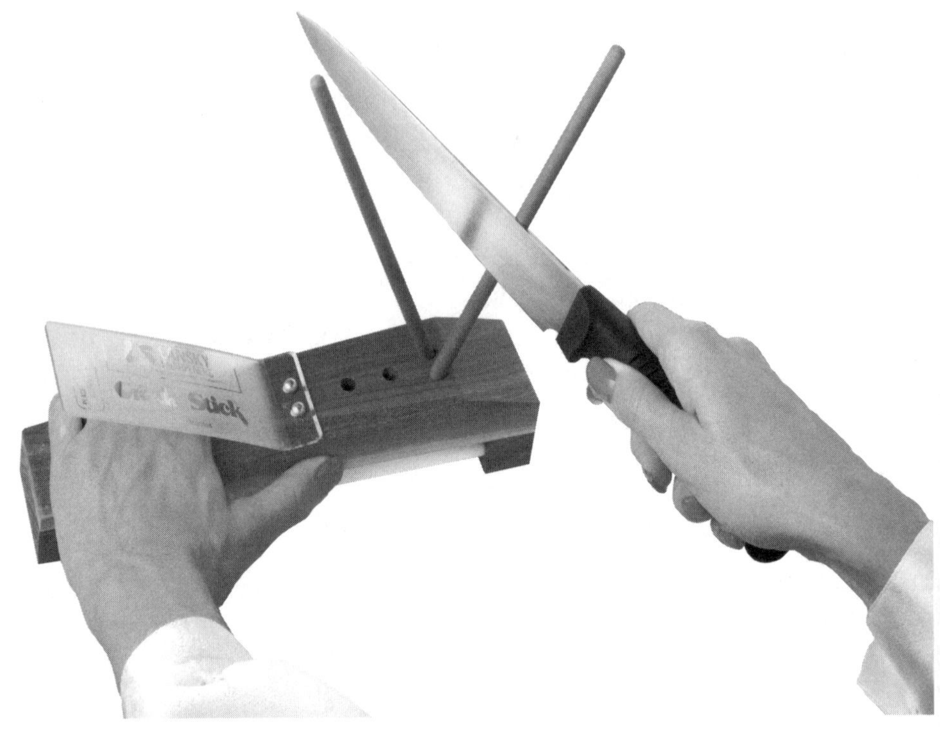

Crock Sticks are convenient for use in the kitchen.

Unfortunately, many of these sharpeners come with only one abrasive grade of rods, so they have limited use. A set with two or three different sets of rods is much more versatile. The Spyderco TriAngle SharpMaker comes with two sets of ceramic rods and a third diamond set is available. The triangular rods and many configurations made this a very versatile sharpener. It can be used to sharpen scissors, darts, fishhooks, serrated blades, etc.

Small ceramic rods with wooden handles are useful for sharpening serrated knives, or carrying in the field for quick touchups. They are available in several abrasive grades. Ceramic sticks without handles are available very cheaply if you want to make your own.

This sharpener works like Crock Sticks, but folds for easy carrying.

Slot Gadgets

There are a whole lot of gadgets on the market that promise easy sharpening. They range in price from under $2 to over $50. Theoretically, with slot-type gadgets you just draw the knife through a slot a few times and it will be sharp. I have tried a lot of them. Many are worthless gimmicks, but some are worth considering.

The most primitive type of slot gadget uses a pair of tungsten carbide tool inserts set at an angle. A variation uses a set of overlapping carbide wheels. In the better units the carbide is undercut by a few degrees to create a sharper edge. These devices literally scrape metal away from the edge, and leave a sharp but somewhat ragged edge. They are good for shaping the initial bevel but do not provide any way to hone or polish the edge. Price is your best guide in this category. The good ones are expensive, and the cheap ones are usually poor. You get what you pay for.

The better slot gadgets use ceramic wheels or rods. Some use two sets, medium and fine. These hone well but they are limited in their ability to sharpen because they cannot remove much metal. They are very handy to keep in the kitchen or shop for quick touchups between sharpenings.

An even better slot gadget uses diamond hones. The fast cutting action of the diamond hones makes them somewhat more useful than the ceramic units.

If you are going to benefit from a slot gadget, it must hone (sharpen) at an equal or greater angle than your existing edge. If the slot angle is less than the existing edge angle, the stones will never contact the edge. Several makers of electric sharpeners also make a matching slot gadget that is useful for touch-ups.

The best slot gadget I have found, the Meyerco Sharpen-It, features tungsten carbide wheels in the first stage and ceramic wheels in the second. The ceramic is so hard and fine-grained that it is almost like using a steel. With this combination, the Sharpen-It performs well at both sharpening and honing.

Unlike other slot devices, the Sharpen-It adds a third wheel to each set, giving it two slots. The wheels are shaped so that they

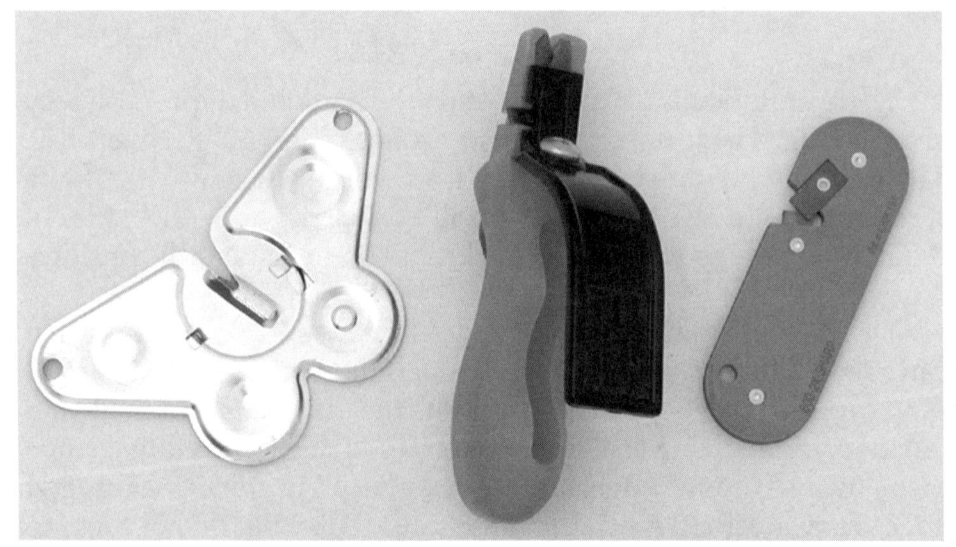

For tungsten carbide slot devices, quality seems to be proportional to price. The cheap ones use straight cutters of low grade TC, while the better ones use profiled cutters of the best TC grade.

Klawhorn Industries makes these slot devices with profiled tungsten carbide cutters and handles coated with a ceramic abrasive.

sharpen one side of the blade at a time. This setup allows you to vary the bevel angle somewhat. Drawing the knife through at an angle decreases the bevel angle and gives a more razor-like edge. Also, unlike others, the Sharpen-It can be used equally well left-handed. It is so compact when closed that it can be carried in the watch pocket of your jeans. The current version includes a tapered hone for serrated blades.

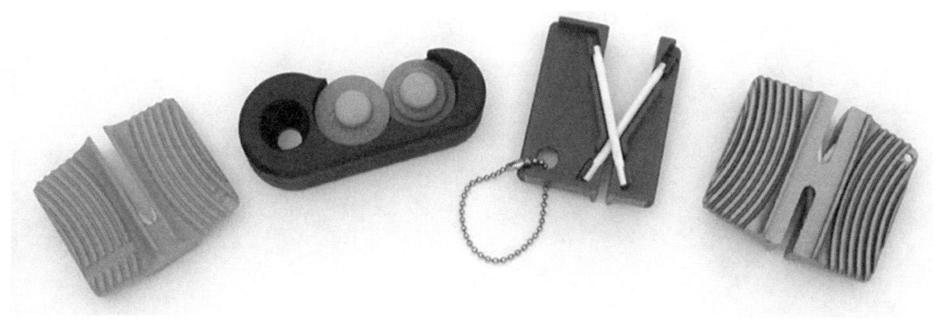

Ceramic slot devices have limited sharpening ability but are handy for touch-ups. Try a cheap one.

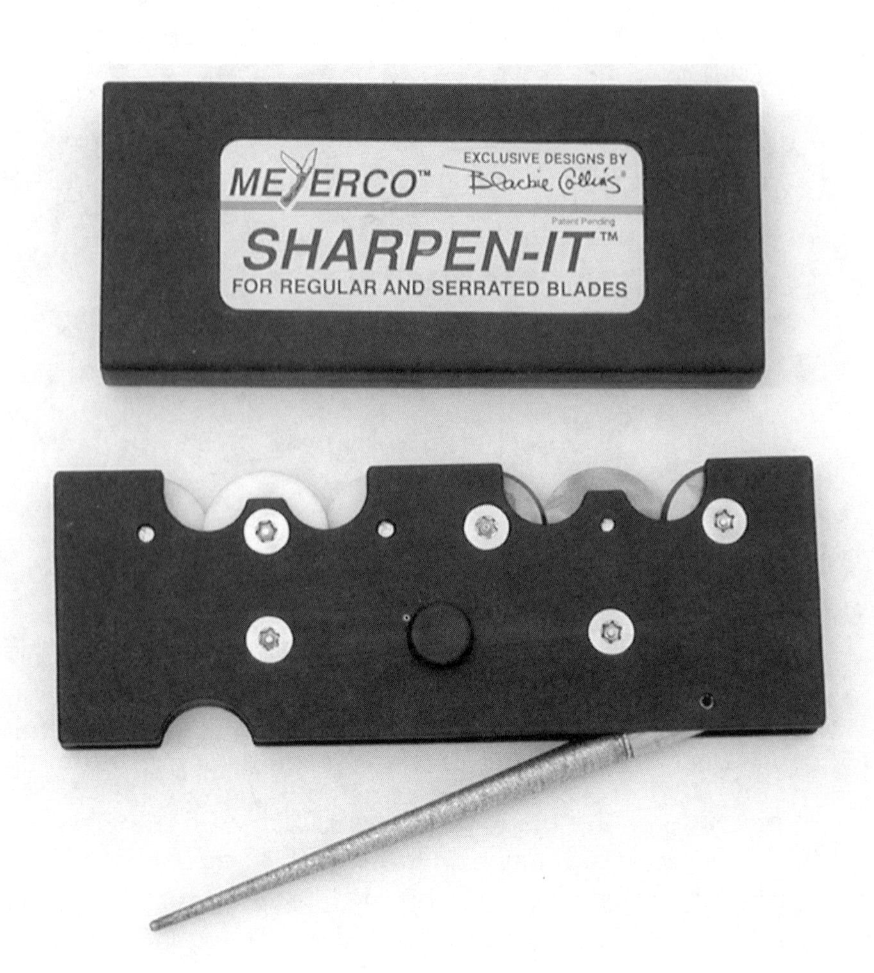

The Sharpen-It combines profiled tungsten carbide cutters and ceramic stones to make a complete sharpening system. The diamond-coated rod is for serrated blades.

Using Sharpening Machines

Electric Sharpening Machines

You probably plan to sharpen your knives by hand. However, if you have no mechanical skills or want to recommend sharpening devices to others, you might want to consider a home electric sharpener. If you plan on running a sharpening business, a labor saving commercial machine will make the difference between a profitable business and a labor of love.

Cheap electric knife sharpeners, like those which are found on can openers, grind aggressively but with little control of angle or depth. I've seen many knives ruined by them and they have given electric sharpeners a bad reputation. Quality machines designed exclusively for knife sharpening are now available, and they are *much* better.

Some designs feature four interleaved, counter-rotating wheels. Commercial machines of this design have adjustable angles, which makes them more expensive. These machines tend to cut very fast so they cut down on the knife's useful life. They also produce a concave edge, which starts off very sharp, but is fragile and dulls faster than a flat or convex grind. I have not been impressed with this type of sharpener, although I have not tried the commercial machines.

The better machines are multi-stage, and use a slower grinding method. Some feature either orbital motion or water cooled/lubricated stones.

The Chef'sChoice™ line of sharpeners ranges from two and three stage home machines to commercial models with replaceable abrasive heads. The newest machines have conical grinders that produce a multi-bevel edge with flat bevels and a polymer strop that produces razor sharpness. After reviewing over 45 sharpening systems, Chef'sChoice™ is my recommendation in this category.

The current models of Chef'sChoice sharpeners feature a polymer strop that gives a razor edge.

Wet Wheel Machines

Eventually you will want to remove a lot of material from a blade, like removing nicks or re-grinding a broken tip. Trying this on an ordinary bench grinder is likely to overheat the blade, destroying the temper and ruining the knife. If this is a rare occurrence, take the blade to a commercial sharpener.

While a repair can be done with hand stones and a lot of patience, if you want to be able to do it quickly and easily, a wet wheel machine is the way to go. Water prevents overheating the blade and ruining the temper, no matter how much you grind. Wet wheel machines are also excellent for general purpose sharpening.

There are two basic styles - vertical wheels where the grinding is done on the perimeter, and horizontal wheels where the grinding is done on the side of the wheel. Horizontal wheels produce a flat grind. Since the wheel is held in by gravity, it is easy to change the wheel for another of a different grit. They usually provide guides for planer and jointer blades and other woodworking tools, and therefore are popular with woodworkers.

Vertical machines with small wheels, 3 inches or less, are available for less than $50. They produce a concave grind, but it can easily be removed with a flat stone. A small wet wheel machine is a good buy if you have a small budget. Vertical wheel machines with 10-inch wheels cost between $150 and $250, and their concavity is hardly different than a flat grind.

The inexpensive 10" wet wheel machines mentioned above have

This large wet wheel sharpener from Tormek includes a leather strop.

a limited number of guides or fixtures available, mostly for planer and joiner knives. The wet wheel grinding system with the most complete set of guides and fixtures for all sharpening needs is the Tormek. The basic machine is about $400, and the average jig is about $40. An indispensable accessory is the Tormek stone grader that changes the stone's texture, which has the same effect as changing the grit. Figure on spending $500 just to sharpen knives, and up to $900 to cover all the woodworking tools. While it is expensive, it is unmatched in its versatility.

Paper Wheels

If you are comfortable using power tools, try a paper wheel system. Paper wheels are somewhat safer than buffing wheels because they are less likely to catch and throw a knife, but you must still work with the wheels moving off the edge for safety. Because the wheel is moving off the edge, it can cause a non-locking folding knife to snap closed, so be sure your fingers are safely positioned on the sides of the handle.

Paper wheels used on a modified bench grinder make a very effective sharpening system.

Paper wheels are often seen demonstrated at gun and knife shows, and are also available from knifemaking supply shops and woodworking tool stores. Two wheels are generally used, which mount on a bench grinder or buffer. The sharpening wheel is coated with silicon carbide, and low melting point grease is used to cool the blade. Buffing compound is used on the other wheel for honing. The sharpening wheel raises a burr quickly. The honing wheel polishes the burr off and leaves a mirror finish comparable to stropping by hand.

Using paper wheels requires a little skill, but once you get the hang of it, it is very fast. Average time to sharpen a kitchen knife is about one minute.

I use paper wheels a little differently than recommended by the manufacturer. Normally a grinding wheel turns toward the user and grinding is done on the front, while debris is thrown downward. The instructions for paper wheels say to use this same rotation but sharpen on top, where debris is thrown toward you. This seems inherently unsafe to me, since the whole knife could be caught and thrown at you.

Here is how I modify a bench grinder for safer use of paper wheels.

I recommend buying a bench grinder to dedicate for this purpose, as changing the wheels too often can introduce wobble in them. When buying a grinder, make sure it has removable guards, because the guards must be taken off. Buy a 6-inch grinder to use 8″ paper wheels, or an 8-inch grinder to use 10″ wheels. The extra clearance is needed when sharpening long blades.

I mount the grinder backwards, so that the top of the wheels move away from me, and sharpen and hone on top of the wheel with the edge facing away. This lets me see better, and debris or anything caught by the wheel is thrown away from me. I hold the blade level and work near the top for a small angle, down the wheel closer to me for a larger angle.

I've marked angles of 0, 15, 20 and 25 degrees on my wheel. When the blade is held horizontally, the angle between the blade and the wheel (angle A) is equal to the angle between the point of contact and vertical (angle B). I put zero at the top and position the blade at the angle mark I want to grind before I start the motor. Then I turn it on and hold the angle steady as I move the knife lengthwise. Practice a little and you will learn how to hold the blade to get the proper angle. If you are not sure you are sharpening at the correct angle you can use the black marker technique introduced on p. 40-41.

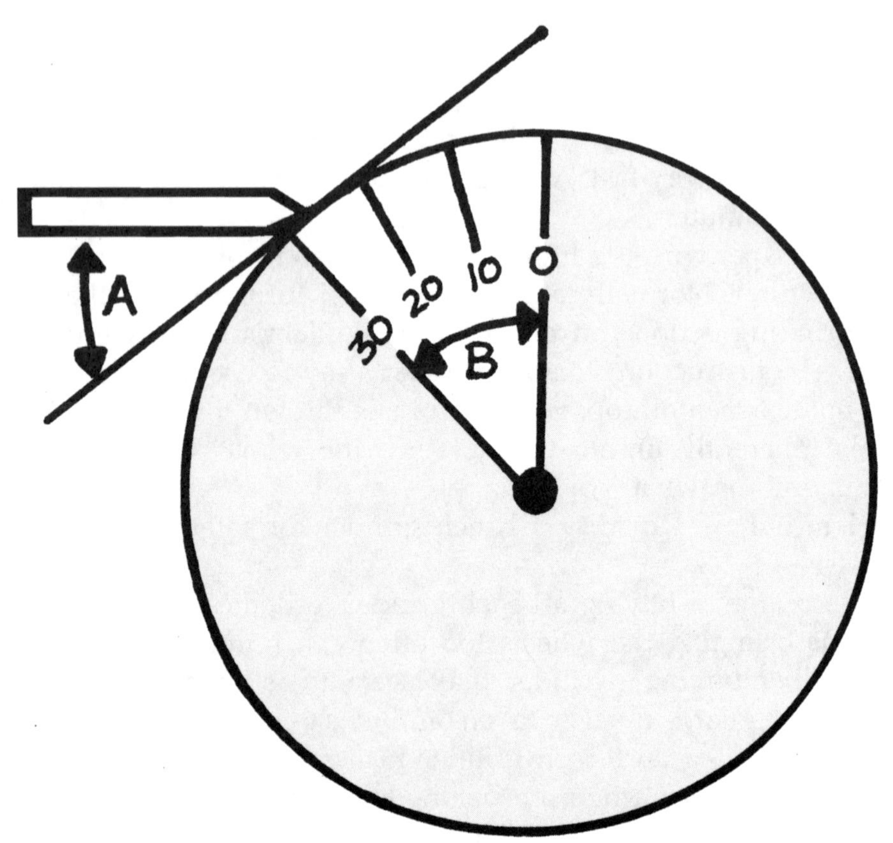

The angle marks on this wheel allow an estimate of the bevel angle (angle A = angle B). Here, the wheel rotates clockwise.

This method seems to produce a sharp edge even when the angle is not tightly controlled. Put a good light over the grinder so you can see the burr as it develops, then polishes away.

Woodworking catalogs offer a variety of rubberized, nylon and composite buffing wheels for sharpening. These were originally made for deburring and polishing, but do a great job sharpening as well. They require skill and practice, and they are expensive. Paper wheels are a better choice for the home knife sharpener.

Belt Sanders

The belt sander is a popular sharpening tool, often seen in knife shops and shows. The knifemaker's grinder, basically a powerful belt sander that takes a 2 inch by 72 inch belt, can be used for sharpening, but sanders with 1 inch by 30 inch or 1 inch by 42 inch belts allow more maneuvering room, and their slower speed reduces the chances of overheating the blade.

A guide for sharpening is available that fits most 1 inch belt sanders, and there is also a leather belt available for stropping.

The procedure is much the same as any sharpening technique – start at about 300 grit for the initial bevel, then step to 600 grit for the next bevel. As with any abrasive on a flexible or soft backing, the abrasive must move off the edge to avoid the blade catching on the belt. Some sharpeners like to use a worn 600 grit belt for the final step. It leaves an edge smoother than a new belt, but with enough tooth to cut fibrous material well. Proceed to a finer belt or a leather strop if you prefer a polished edge.

Conclusion

Congratulations and thank you for reading this far. Hopefully this book, combined with some practice, will enable you to get a sharp edge on your knives and other household tools. Enjoy the pleasure of using your tools, and the satisfaction of knowing *you* made them sharp.

The information in this book came from many sources in addition to my own experience. If you want to study further, I recommend reading any of the books in the bibliography, especially the first one, *The Complete Guide to Sharpening* by Leonard Lee. Although it focuses on woodworking tools, it has a chapter on knives and a very good explanation of sharpening theory.

There is also a lot of information on knife sharpening available on the Internet. I maintain a website at www.SharpeningMadeEasy.com where I review sharpening systems and have links to other sharpening information. I can also be reached by e-mail at steve@sharpeningmadeeasy.com.

Appendices

Care and Safety

"Don't run with scissors." "Cut away from yourself." Since childhood we have been warned of the dangers of using and handling sharp tools. And it is true, sharp instruments involve some risk. A childhood friend was badly cut by a wood chisel when it simply fell from the bench as my friend stood watching the sharpener work. It pays to be careful with sharp tools.

Common sense tells us a sharp knife or tool can cut quickly and deeply. I want to mention a few things that common sense, or even our mothers, may not have told us.

A dull tool can be even more dangerous than a sharp one. A dull knife requires more pressure and is therefore more likely to cause an accident by slipping. A sharp knife allows more deliberate, controlled cuts.

Try to avoid cutting toward yourself or another person when possible. When it is necessary to cut toward yourself, as when butchering a large carcass, cut with your arm straight and pull with your shoulder. If the knife slips or comes free, your whole body will move back with it.

Kitchen knives with square (German-style) handles have the unfortunate ability to lay on their back with the edge up. Knives with round (French-style) handles will roll over on their sides, which is safer. French knives are much less popular in the American market than German ones, but one American maker, Chef'sChoice™, uses the French-style handle.

Knives should be washed soon after their use, before material dries on them. If you cannot wash them right away, they should at least be wiped clean to reduce the amount of dried material that has to be washed off later.

Never wash knives in a dishwasher, which bangs them around

and dulls the edges. Also, never leave knives in the dishwater. It is far too easy to hit the sharp edge when feeling for the unseen knife in the sink. This is doubly dangerous when the knife is the square German type mentioned above. My worst cut came from striking my knuckle on such a submerged knife.

The safest way to wash a knife is to hold it in one hand while washing it with the other. Wash the edge by reaching around the spine of the knife with a dishcloth or sponge, and pinching the blade between your thumb and forefinger. This way the knife cannot cut the web of the thumb, and the thumb and finger will guide the dishcloth safely along the edge. Rinse the knife while still holding it and dry it like you washed it before placing it in a safe place and starting to wash another knife.

Knives should be stored in a block or holder that keeps them separated and allows air to circulate around the blade in case it is put away damp. Never throw them loose in a drawer.

Sheath knives should also be stored in a block, holder or box. Knives stored in a leather sheath will corrode and/or rust. Knives stored for a long time, especially non-stainless knives, should be coated with a protective coating like silicone oil that will not attract moisture.

Folding knives should be cleaned and lubricated as part of the sharpening process. Penetrating oils like WD-40™ work okay, but the residue tends to attract dust. It is better to clean folding knives with a pure solvent, then lubricate them with a teflon or wax-based lubricant that does not attract dust.

Always wear safety glasses when working with power equipment, and when using a buffing wheel or a ScotchBrite™ belt, also consider wearing a heavy leather apron and cut-proof gloves.

Blade Materials

Knife blades are traditionally made from steel, which is an alloy of iron with carbon and other elements. The steels used in knives are called high carbon steels and typically have a carbon content of 0.5

to 2%. This steel is relatively easy to shape by forging or grinding, and can be heat-treated to hardnesses suitable for knives. Straight high carbon steel takes an excellent edge, but it has little resistance to corrosion.

Most knives today are made from some form of stainless steel. Stainless steel is made by adding 12% or more chromium to the alloy, which gives it corrosion resistance. Stainless steel blades not only look nice longer, but also will hold an edge longer in wet conditions. Other elements added to steel to improve hardness, toughness and wear resistance are cobalt, manganese, molybdenum, nickel and vanadium. Increasing any of these properties makes the blade a little harder to shape and sharpen, but there is a payback in increased usefulness. The term "surgical stainless steel" is meaningless, because many different stainless steels are used for surgical instruments.

The most popular stainless steels used in today's blades are from the 420 and 440 families. 420 stainless is often used in fantasy and other low cost knives because it is cheap and corrosion resistant, but it cannot be hardened enough to make a good working knife. A typical kitchen knife will be made from higher carbon 420HC or 440A steel. They are easy to sharpen and have moderately good edge retention. 440C is an excellent compromise of price and performance and is used by many custom and production makers. 440C is slightly more difficult to sharpen than the others, but has better edge retention.

If you buy specialty cutlery or a custom made knife, you will have more steels to choose from. ATS-34 is used by custom makers and by a few production makers, notably Benchmade. Among steels, CPM-440V is the edge retention champion, but it is difficult to sharpen. BG-42 challenges CPM-440V in edge retention, and is as easy to sharpen as 440C. Only a few custom makers are using CPM-440V and BG-42 at this time.

Powdered metal technology makes it possible to incorporate higher percentages of alloying elements than will stay in solution in molten steel. Increasing desirable elements like carbon and vanadium has created a whole new family of steels like CPM-440V mentioned above. CPM stands for Crucible Particle Metallurgy, and they are the pioneers in this area. Watch for new knives produced with steels from CPM.

Knife steels are heat treated to control their hardness. Steel hardness is measured on a device called a Rockwell hardness tester. Knife blades may vary from about 55 to 62 on the Rockwell C scale. In general, blades under 55 Rc are easy to sharpen but do not hold an edge well. Blades over 60 Rc are difficult to sharpen, and may chip in hard use unless the alloy is very tough. 55 to 59 Rc is a good range for kitchen knives.

Using combinations of heating and cooling, the maker tries to get the perfect temper, a balance between hardness and strength. You want enough hardness for wear resistance without being brittle. During cooling the steel forms different compounds, depending on the cooling rate. Fast cooling or "quenching" from a high temperature forms harder compounds. Cryogenic treatment, freezing with liquid nitrogen or dry ice, can speed these transitions and improve the grain structure. Slow cooling allows softer compounds to form. Annealing, a slow cooling from an intermediate temperature, is used after quenching to complete transitions in the steel that would normally take place over time, creating a more stable blade. Annealing also provides fine control of the hardness.

Sometimes differential heat-treating is used to combine a hard edge with a tough spine. Mechanical methods can be used to create this same effect. Laminated steel, with a hard core that becomes the edge surrounded by tough outer layers, is available in both regular and stainless. The samurai sword is a well-known example of both differential heat treatment and mechanical layering.

Laminated steel is different than Damascus steel. Laminated steel has all the layers parallel to the edge for strength and hardness. Damascus steel has the layers at various angles, and is often chosen for decorative effect.

Another approach to knife steels has been taken by knifemaker

David Boye. His knives are made from cast stainless steel. Boye's steel has a matrix of carbide dendrites that are exposed to form a micro-saw when sharpened. These carbides are highly wear resistant. Boye is also making cast cobalt alloy knives.

The search for edge retention has led knifemakers to try wear resistant materials like Vascowear. Vascowear is a high vanadium steel that was developed for industrial knives subject to high wear.

Another wear resistant material is Stellite, a cobalt alloy with about 30% chromium, 3% or less iron and 1 to 3% of other elements. Since it contains so little iron, it is technically not steel but a cobalt-chromium alloy. Stellite tests at a low Rockwell C hardness, about 38 to 40, but it contains harder carbides that do the cutting and retain the edge. Stellite will tie or beat CPM-440V for edge-retention, but it is very difficult to sharpen. A cobalt-chromium-tungsten alloy named Talonite is similar to Stellite. Both alloys cannot be heat-treated and are non-magnetic.

Titanium is known mainly for making lightweight, high-strength fasteners for aerospace use, but it is also used for knife blades. Titanium is favored for salt water diving because of its excellent corrosion resistance. Like Stellite and Talonite, titanium has a low Rockwell C hardness, but it has good wear resistance and requires diamond hones to sharpen. Titanium is also non-magnetic.

Ceramic materials exhibit very high hardness and wear resistance. Boker, Kyocera and others make knives with ceramic blades.

In the future, expect to see surface coatings take a greater role in blade technology. It is now possible to coat extremely hard materials like carbides, nitrides, ceramics and even diamond onto steel. This can dramatically improve edge retention, and application of these materials to only one side can result in a blade that is self sharpening like a beaver's tooth. And don't think the underlying material will always be steel. Carbon and ceramic fibers have some superior characteristics that I would love to see incorporated into knife blades.

Sharpening Materials

While steel hardness is measured on the Rockwell C scale, the materials used for sharpening are measured on another hardness scale, one intended for minerals. It is called the Mohs scale after its inventor, Friedrich Mohs. The original Mohs scale ran from 1 for talc to 10 for diamond. Scientists have introduced a new Mohs scale, but it has not caught on. The new scale spreads out the scale between silica and diamond to make it more closely equal to physical hardness (on the new scale, diamond is 15). Because the Mohs and Rockwell scales use different methods they cannot be compared directly, but knife steel is roughly 5.5 on Mohs scale and files are roughly 6. A chart below compares the old and new Mohs scale.

NOTE: References to Mohs hardness throughout the text of this book utilize the "old" Mohs scale.

MOHS HARDNESS SCALE

OLD	NEW	EXAMPLE
1	1	talc
2	2	gypsum
3	3	calcite
3.5	3.5	copper penny
4	4	florspar (florite)
5	5	apatite
5.5	5.5	glass, knife steel
6	6	orthoclase, file steel
6.5		novaculite (silicon dioxide)*
7	8	vitreous pure silica, quartz*
8	9	topaz
10		garnet
11		fused zirconium oxide
9		sapphire or corundum*
9.2	12	fused alumina*
9.4	13	silicon carbide*
9.6	14	boron carbide
9.8		cubic boron nitride*
10	15	diamond*

**Common sharpening abrasives*

Comparing Abrasive Grits

Grit sizes of belts, wheels and stones used in knife sharpening			
Stones and hones	Grit size (mesh)	Japanese waterstones	Average grit size in microns
Coarse Crystolon	100	150	140
	120		116
Medium Crystolon, coarse India	150		92
	180	240	77
	220		66
Extra coarse diamond hone			60
Medium India, fine Crystolon	240	280	53
Coarse diamond			46
Fine India	280	360	44
Medium diamond	320	500	36
Washita	360	600	29
Fine diamond			25
	400		24
Soft Arkansas	500	1000	20
	600		16
Hard white Arkansas, extra fine diamond, and medium ceramic	700	2000	14
DMT "1200" extra-fine diamond hone			9
Hard black Arkansas	1000	4000	9
	1200		6.5
	1500		6
	2000		5
Extra fine white ceramic, green chrome rouge		6000	3
Japanese waterstone		8000	2
Chromium oxide polishing compound			0.5
Crystolon™ is Norton Abrasives trade mark for Silicon Carbide stones			
India™ is Norton Abrasives trade mark for Aluminum Oxide stones			

A larger version of this chart is available at
http://users.ameritech.net/knives/grit.htm

Suppliers of Sharpening Equipment

DMT (Diamond Machining Technology)
85 Hayes Memorial Dr.
Marlborough, MA 01752
(508) 481-5944
DMT diamond and ceramic sharpening hones
www.dmtsharp.com

EdgeCraft
825 Southwood Rd
Avondale, PA 19311-9727
(610) 268-0500 Customer service (800) 342-3255
Chef'sChoice™ diamond electric and manual sharpeners, Kitchen cutlery
www.edgecraft.com

EdgePal
Jämtland, Sweden
EdgePal sharpening system
www.edgepal.com

EdgePro
PO Box 95
Hood River, OR 97031
(541) 387-2222
EdgePro Apex and Professional rod-guided sharpening system
www.edgeproinc.com

Eze-Lap Diamond Products
3572 Arrowhead Dr.
Carson City, NV 89706
(775) 888-9500
Eze-Lap Diamond sharpening hones
www.eze-lap.com

GATCO
PO Box 600
Getzville, NY 14068-0600
(716) 877-2200
Full line of sharpeners
www.greatamericantool.com

Hall's Arkansas Oilstones, Inc.
3800 Amity Road
Pearcy, AR 71964
(501) 525-8595
Natural Arkansas stones
www.hallsproedge.com

Klawhorn Industries
456 South Blvd.
Wadsworth, OH 44281
Advanced tungsten carbide slot sharpeners
(330) 335-8191

Lansky Sharpeners
PO Box 800
Buffalo, NY 14231-0800
(716) 877-7511
Full line of sharpeners
www.lansky.com

McGowan Manufacturing
4854 N. Shamrock Place
Tucson, AZ 85705
(800) 342-4810
FireStone and DiamondStone Electric and manual sharpeners
www.mcgowanmfg.com

Meyerco
4481 Exchange Service Dr.
Dallas, TX 75236
(214) 467-8949
Blackie Collins designs including the Sharpen-It slot sharpener
www.meyercousa.com

Razor Edge Systems, Inc.
303 N 17th Ave E
Ely, MN 55731
(218) 365-6419
Razor Edge sharpening systems
www.razoredgesystems.com

Razor Sharp Edgemaking System
P.O. Box 6554
Eureka, CA 95502
(877) 725-2197
Paper Wheel systems
www.sharpeningwheels.com

SKARB
2427 Richley Road
Corfu, NY 14036
(585) 547-9388
Unique rod-guided sharpening system
www.skarb.com

Spyderco, Inc.
PO Box 800
Golden, CO 80402-0800
(303) 279-8383
Cutlery and Ceramic stones, including Tri-Angle SharpMaker ceramic rod system
www.spyderco.com

Tormek
Lindesberg, Sweden
www.tormek.se
Wet wheel grinding and honing system

Warthog Sharpeners-USA
10791 N.W. 53rd St # 115
Sunrise, FL 33351
(954) 275-6872
Warthog V-Sharp and Hunter sharpeners
www.warthogsharp.com

Bibliography

(1) The Complete Guide to Sharpening by Leonard Lee
Taunton Books; ISBN 1-56158-125-9; $22.95
A great book on sharpening; it covers woodworking tools as well as knives.
Lots of technical material including electron microscope photographs.

(2) The Razor Edge Book of Sharpening by John Juranitch
Warner Books; ISBN 0-446-38002-4; $19.95
Mostly on knives, plus how to sharpen some sportsman's tools.
Available from Knife World, Razor Edge Systems, and some knifemaking suppliers.

(3) Sharpening with Waterstones by Ian Kirby
Cambium Press; ISBN 0964399938; $14.95
Mostly for woodworkers with only three pages on knives, but more on waterstones than I've found anywhere else.

(4) Step by Step Knifemaking by David Boye
Boye Knives; ISBN: 0615116590; $21.95
Covers sharpening with a belt grinder and buffer, as well as manual sharpening and stropping.

(5) Sharpening Basics by Patrick Spielman
Sterling Publishing; ISBN 0-8069-7226-2; $9.95
Good chapter on knives, but measures angles from the edge rather than the center line.

(6) Sharpening - The Complete Guide by Jim Kingshott
Guild of Master Craftsman Publications; ISBN 0-946819-48-3; $17.95
Good theory, but very little on knives.

photo by Pollack Studio

Author Steve Bottorff is retired from a career that started in engineering and ended in sales and marketing. He and wife and son lived in Japan for 3 years, and Steve is interested in Japanese swords and cutlery. Fifteen years ago he began seriously investigating knife sharpening. Frustrated by the inconsistent results he got on different knives, he began purchasing and testing a wide variety of sharpening devices. With time, he was able to identify the keys to success, and he has written this book so that everyone can learn how to sharpen a knife to a razor edge. Steve is a member of the Ohio Knifemakers Association and the Western Reserve Cutlery Association. His website is www.SharpeningMadeEasy.com, and he can be contacted by e-mail at steve@SharpeningMadeEasy.com.